T0301205

THE COVE

Also by Beth Lynch

Where the Hornbeam Grows

THE COVE

A Cornish Haunting

BETH LYNCH

WEIDENFELD & NICOLSON

First published in Great Britain in 2024 by Weidenfeld & Nicolson
an imprint of The Orion Publishing Group Ltd
Carmelite House, 50 Victoria Embankment
London EC4Y 0DZ
An Hachette UK Company

1 3 5 7 9 10 8 6 4 2

Extracts from 'Morwenstow' and 'The Forest of Tangle' from *Collected Poems 1951–2000* by Charles Causley (Picador), reproduced by permission of David Higham Associates
Extracts from 'The Listeners' by Walter de la Mare reproduced by permission of The Literary Trustees of Walter de la Mare and the Society of Authors

A CIP catalogue record for this book is
available from the British Library.

ISBN (Hardback) 9781474606936
ISBN (eBook) 9781474606967

Typeset by Input Data Services Ltd, Bridgwater, Somerset

Printed in Great Britain by Clays Ltd, Elcograf, S.p.A.

MIX
Paper from
responsible sources
FSC
www.fsc.org
FSC® C104740

www.weidenfeldandnicolson.co.uk
www.orionbooks.co.uk

This book is dedicated to Shaun

and

to my parents' memory

revenant. 1. One who returns from the dead; a ghost.
2. One who returns to a place.

Oxford English Dictionary

When will you rest, sea?
> *When moon and sun*
> *Ride only fields of salt water*
> *And the land is gone.*

Charles Causley

Contents

Prologue

My mother is watching the night from a hospital window. The seaside town shimmers below, a sodium constellation. Beyond, in darkness, lone lights bob and wink or inch horizontally leftwards, rightwards. Above it all burns a waxing crescent moon.

The nursery ward smells of disinfectant and other people's babies. Night lights and a desk lamp make the room darkly visible. My mother looks around quickly – no nurse in sight, the serried cots, the neat blanketed slumbering mounds – and with her free hand unfastens the catch. She opens the window wide and breathes in the night: the late-August cool, the dull salinity of the English Channel. Her other arm cradles a newborn girl.

It has just gone two. Soon twenty-four hours will have passed since my mother gave birth in the hospital on the hill. Who knows what she went through bringing this baby into the world; she must be sore, exhausted, enchanted. She studies the sleeping features in the silver-sepia light. The frowning and puckering and letting go; the translucent eyelids, their periodic flutterings; the pursing of lips and sucking of prospective teeth as if some dream were being dreamed, some existential question wrestled with. The little face looks ages older than itself. Hello, my mother says as the eyes snap open. She inhales the smell of the silky head and lifts the baby upright.

The footsteps were inevitable. Tap-tap-tap-tap, authority on linoleum. The night sister shuts the window – it is no mean feat to do this assertively in a roomful of sleeping infants – and reaches for the baby and, reconsidering, settles for a gesture: just what does my mother think she is doing?? Drawn as by magnetic force, she has got out of her bed in the maternity ward, put on her slippers and candlewick dressing gown, walked straight down the corridor to the nursery ward, and picked up her baby. Without permission.

I'm showing my daughter the lights, my mother says evenly.

The sister pauses. First-timers are mostly young, mostly deferential, they lack confidence. They want you to tell them what is what. This woman is in her mid-thirties and, as of very early yesterday morning, a mother of three. She knows a thing or two about babies. She knows that newborns cannot see very far at all, a few inches or so. She stands at the window, looking out, as if the nurse does not exist, as if mother and child are the only beings in the room, the world. Treading softly this time, the nurse withdraws to the desk by the door and pretends to read notes beneath a low lamp.

The moon, my mother murmurs, look at the moon. See the streetlights down there. There's the pier. There's a car. The infant stares unfathomably, taking in everything and nothing in particular. And that's a boat, my mother whispers, looking at a far-off winking light. She tells the baby about the sea. About the tides and the pull of the moon. About a place of Atlantic waves and tumultuous cliffs and salt-bright air. Where there are red-legged oystercatchers, thrift and seaweed, rocky coves.

The baby knows the place in every last salt-watery cell of her newborn being. She has been there before.

The photograph was taken a few months earlier, on a boat trip out of Padstow. In the foreground my mother is sitting on a slatted bench. Next to her, slightly out of focus and enthralled by something we cannot see, are a boy and a girl, one of whom is not quite six, the other four and a bit. They are holding hands. The skipper is at the wheel behind them, a cigarette in his steering hand. In background haze is the craggy outline of Rumps Point and, a little off the headland, Puffin Island.

It's my mother who is the subject of the photograph, perfectly lit, perfectly in focus: my father, behind the camera, is captivated by her and it is not difficult to see why. Impeccably lipsticked, her dark crop windswept, chic in her lovely tweed coat, she is gazing off out to sea, far away beyond the frame, and smiling to herself. Her right arm cradles a just-discernible bump.

We are well into September now. My mother brought the baby home a week or two ago. Paternity leave is a thing of the future, but my father digs deep for my brother and sister, putting their importance out of doubt: there are adventures in the wood, bicycles and board games, conversations, stories read together. In quiet moments he picks up the baby and wanders out into the garden. He shows her flowers and the fall of early-autumn light on leaves. The waning phases of the moon. He sings a song from across the Atlantic –

I's the b'y that builds the boat
And I's the b'y that sails her

– and the baby is carried in the rhythm of his steps and his voice.

The Japanese anemones are still in flower. My mother loves Japanese anemones. The baby sleeps on her shoulder while she snips away spent blooms, and as she reaches in with the secateurs pink petals brush the little head like butterfly wings.

She will always be the little sister by a mile, the youngest in her school year too, this baby born on the edge of summer. She sleeps so-so and feeds well, almost too well some would say, and yet something is not quite right. Once or twice, for no obvious reason, my mother tells the district nurse, the baby has frozen rigid in her arms. The spasms last for five, ten seconds though they feel like an eternity, and then everything seems right as rain. Could it be epilepsy, or worse?

The nurse has seen this before. The baby feels that she's going to fall, some kind of fear instinct. It's not especially common, but certainly no cause for concern. Thank goodness: seizure disorders, brain tumours, all sorts of things have been hurtling through my mother's mind. And yet the explanation cuts her to the quick: how can this tiny girl be afraid of falling when her parents hold her so in their love? Will she grow out of it, my mother asks the nurse. Oh yes: the spasms will tail off in time. Give it a few months, be patient.

What about the fear?

The fear?

Yes. Will she grow out of the fear too?

Maybe, my father says later, it's like when you jolt yourself awake just as you are dropping off.

You are falling asleep and then you are falling.

I

Seasons in the Sun

Everybody needs a cove, a recess in the world. Mine is on the edge of Cornwall, where the Atlantic Ocean's perpetual advance meets towering, slipping metamorphic rock. My cove is an in-between place. It is land and it is sea. It owes its shape to the elements, and to humanity. It is enclosed by walls of slate and open to immensity:

There's the sea! I can see the sea!

It is said that those were my first complete sentences. I have little or no recollection of my earliest encounters with the cove at the end of the 1960s; that time belongs to dreams and the margins of things. When I summon up anecdotes that my parents told me, or rifle through an inherited stash of Agfa transparencies, it is as if they bear witness to another person's life – yet, with a bodily certainty that I cannot explain, I know that I was there. I have haunted the place ever since. For fifty years and counting I have returned, again and again, on paths that twist deep between hedgebanks, stretch over clifftops scoured by wind, disappear into gorse. Paths that bump and jolt through cow-churned valleys and keep company with streams. Paths traversing interior landscapes; paths recalled and paths followed feelingly.

There's the sea! I can see the sea!

I am taking one of those paths right now, going back to the cove. Actually, it is my father who is striding along the cliff path; I am riding high on his shoulders. I'm three-and-a-half years old and on top of the world. You are never too young to appreciate the salt wind in your face and hair, the blue sky and the deep-blue glittering sea. Everything is bright and airy and singing, not singing as my father is singing now, nor as birds sing, but just, well, singing. I will never, at a more articulate age, be able to explain quite what I mean by this, only that it's how I experience the world in all my senses at this moment, in the moment. The path mostly runs through grass, but once or twice we turn a corner and there is nothing but blue to our left, far below and yet so close, and when I look down my stomach heaves a little with the waves.

I's the b'y that builds the boat / And I's the b'y that sails her . . . The path is dry and slightly bouncy so that we are just flying along, and my father's steps keep time with our song. I cannot see my mother nor my siblings in this memory, but I know that my mother is way out in front and that Treacle, our brindle Boxer, is racing back and forth, hurrying everyone along. Treacle is my very best friend. I also have two imaginary friends, Helen and Miranda – my big sister has friends of the same name – but Treacle is real and I love her to bits. *I's the b'y that catches the fish / And brings 'em home to LI-ZA*: my father tugs my ankles for emphasis. He is also carrying a large blue backpack and, strapped to the top of the pack, a rolled-up stripy blanket on which I am partially sitting. It seems totally natural that my father should carry me as well: he could carry the whole world on his shoulders if he wanted to. I do not think I am particularly comfortable – it's bumpy up here, and although my father is holding my ankles I have to work to keep my balance – but, as I said, I'm on top of the world. *I's the by that bys the by*, I sing tunelessly and uncomprehendingly at the top of my voice.

We pass a tower in a wide green field. A great many rabbit holes, and vivid droppings. My father puts me down for a bit. The grass feels springy beneath my feet, and there's the sea, and clean bright light, and there are seagulls on the air. The things for investigation are too small and too numerous to be stored by a three-and-a-half-year-old brain. Thrift and butterflies, undoubtedly; a wisp of sheep's wool snagged in barbed wire; puff balls, gorse, a lovely cow (there is almost always a lovely cow).

I am wearing an indigo dress that my mother made; I love the colour though I do not yet know its name. It is trimmed with multicoloured braid and very short, with matching knickers, just the thing for clambering over rocks or running around, or riding on shoulders, hobbyhorses, tricycles. My father has picked me up again and we're bumping down a steep, steep hill in great sideways jolting steps. The hillside is in shadow but miles below the sun is blazing and the sea is blue. Now we are making our way along the edge of a stream, a stream like a river: it thunders in my ears. An overhanging tuft gives way underfoot, but my father keeps his balance and I shriek with laughter. This moment will crystallise amongst my earliest memories.

Now it is dark though I am conscious of bright sky overhead. My father is treading carefully, one step at a time, steadying himself with his left hand against a glistening wall of rock. I reach out to touch the wall too, but my fingers recoil from its sliminess. The river runs beside us, and one day I will believe in recollection that above the echoing whoosh I can hear the dark wall trickling.

I am too young to anticipate, to look forward to being in the cove. That will come later: the slippery hurrying down with the stream, down towards the light and the sea, the brimming excitement, almost in the cove. And later still, greater than anticipation, the sheer longing to be there. The cove drawing me back from wherever I happen to be in the world.

This is not to say that there is no excitement in the here and now, frame by frame, moment by thrilling moment, uncomplicated by what will come next. The stream is roaring. My father's steps are heavy and deliberate. The backpack is creaking from side to side, unseating me a little, which makes me giggle. *I's the by that bys the by*: my words are made strange by the dark rocky walls. They stretch and twang and live on in the air. I know that it is slippery underfoot, and I know that my father cannot fall.

The gulley ends in sea-smoothed rock from which, depending on your mood, the weight on your back, the state of your knees, you jump or slither into the cove. A crunch of dense shingle and here you are. Here, in the cove. Light and slate and flooding sound. The iodine pungency of churned kelp. The brightness is almost too much at first, the blue sky and the sky in the sea, the gleaming rocks, the cliffs' slate sheen, but it feels lovely on your face. And there's the sea – right there – the white noise and the cracking waves. The sea on the wind, the salt-vegetal smell: you breathe in deeply, tasting the cove. The stream flows wide amongst the rocks, rushing to oblivion. And from somewhere amongst it all, the sea and the wind, the stream and the water-tumbled stones, the small, clear pip-pip-pip-pip-pip of an oystercatcher sounds in your ears.

*

The great arc of Port Isaac Bay is an uncompromising place. When the light is brisk and blown, as it often is in North Cornwall, this coastline fills me with wonder as if I am seeing it for the very first time. When it is bleak and forbidding it is absolutely so.

A clifftop church marks the northernmost horizon up at Tintagel, a simple silhouette. The tower faces west attentively as though the church were looking or setting out to sea. At the opposite, south-western tip of the bay are the ridged earthworks and ample headland of Rumps Point and, a stone's throw beyond the point, an island, The Mouls: the landscape's full-stop. Anyone who has taken a boat trip out of Padstow will know The Mouls as Puffin Island. Some whose boat was skippered, as mine was, by a certain individual in the 1970s may still believe that the Iron Age ramparts were nothing of the kind, but rather donkey-racing tracks dating from an unspecified period of history.

If you should walk the coast path between Rumps Point and Tintagel Head you will, one way or another, pass by the cove. As for the other cardinal points, Rough Tor (pronounced 'Rowter') lies directly to the east, obscured from the cliff path by the rise of the land; its granite outcrops dominate inland Cornwall and their interstices pulse with prehistoric presence. And if you should put out to sea due west from the cove you would, before you caught up with the setting sun, make landfall on the coast of Newfoundland.

I don't know how to describe it all, I told my mother when I was young. I still don't, but I can list a good few constituent parts. The slate cliffs and sloping headlands. Valleys of varying gradient and of which, however often I walk them, I lose count. Streams and streaming thorny thickets. Watercress, willowherb, marsh marigold. High green fields. Reticulated hedgebanks – Cornish hedges – walled with slate, filled with earth, dense with vegetation. Hawthorn, blackthorn. Curzeyway, the herringbone walling pattern specific to these slaty parts. Sheer slate, hacked slate, laid slate, tumbled slate. Pink campion, bladder campion. Slaty ruins, slate spoil, tracks and holloways. Trodden paths, ghost paths, paths falling over cliffs. Strange stand-alone rock formations. Tumuli. Thrift. And, always, there's the sea.

Apart from Port Isaac's pale sprawl and the tiny hamlet of Trebarwith Strand, these miles of cliff are unpopulated – yet millennia of human life are expressed or stored up in their rocks and thin topsoil. The first Cornish hedges, after all, were Neolithic work. Today the land is managed by farmers and the National Trust, and yet it also feels remote for stretches at a time. The very sight of open ocean cannot but put you in mind of wildness, especially when, so far as you can see, you are alone with the buzzards on a high cliff path. But maybe it also has something to do with that past presence, a human dimension that makes this coast feel old and wild in a unique way. It is different with places that have never been inhabited. A mountain, to my mind at least, is simply ageless.

As recently as the nineteenth century and into the early twentieth these parts were very busy indeed with coastal business. Fishermen plied their trade out of Port Isaac; 'landers' or collectors of sand and seaweed gatherers laboured between tides.

Boats arrived with cargoes of coal and departed laden with roofing slates – and as you walked ever further north the coastline became an industrial landscape. At Tregardock the mining of argentiferous galena is evidenced by broken cliffs, overgrown tracks, chaotic ground and, amongst the bracken and scrub, occasional lengths of curzeyway. Of the coastal slate quarrying that shaped the land's edge a few miles to either side of Tintagel there is, on the other hand, some contemporaneous visual record. The artist Joseph Mallord William Turner, passing through in 1811, made sketches of mutilated cliffs and huge winching frames or poppet heads – a form that seems to have intrigued his eye – from which boulders dangle or slates are lowered to boats moored in Tintagel Haven. 'Slate quarries, one great pillar left standing; ship under the cliff loading', noted Alfred, Lord Tennyson on a ramble from Tintagel in June 1848. Tennyson was not the last future Poet Laureate to be drawn to these cliffs. A century later, long after the quarrymen were gone, the sheds and offices and cutting floors and poppet heads spirited away, John Betjeman described the cliffs around Tintagel in his *Shell Guide* to Cornwall: they look, he wrote without a hint of irony, 'as though man had built them'.

This part of the world captivated my parents not long before my birth. They'd been married for over ten years, a decade consumed financially by a mortgage and two small children. My father had also been seriously ill, and conversations had taken place about how my mother would raise their young family without him. Then there was surgery, then the all-clear, and before they knew it, a baby on the way. And around this time, a time for living life to the full, they decided that they could afford to take their first proper holiday; a Chichester honeymoon cut short due to rain and an inhospitable guest house didn't really count. A friend had spoken enthusiastically about Cornwall, and put them in touch with the proprietors of a holiday let on the north coast. Following correspondence with a certain Mrs Harris my mother booked Flat 1, said to have a sea view, for a week in April at the cost of ten guineas plus metered electricity. My father posted a cheque off to the AA, and eventually received a slender booklet of directions from our home in Sussex to Harlyn Bay, a journey of precisely 307 miles. They left before dawn and arrived at Tamarisk Heights ten-and-three-quarter hours later. My brother and sister were sick in the car.

They unpacked, went straight down to the beach, and later had fried plaice and apple pie for tea. They spent much of the next week investigating beaches. They drove out to Trevose Head, where the lighthouse unfortunately was closed. They went to Padstow and took a boat trip around Rumps Point and Puffin Island. The car broke down and was repaired in Padstow, and broke down again and was fixed in Wadebridge. With the aid of a map drawn by Mrs Harris in black, blue, red and green biro on a quarter-sheet of Basildon Bond, they found their way north to a farm called Tregardock (marked in green), and walked down to a rocky, dark-sanded beach that, my mother recorded, was unbelievably wild. Later, while my father and siblings were busy on the beach, my mother wandered off to explore and think her own thoughts. She struck out on the coast path for a mile or so, came to the top of a steep valley, and found herself looking down on a cove: the cove. At the end of the week my parents booked Flat 1 for the autumn of the following year, by which time the baby ought to be finding his or her feet. It is true that the sea view was, properly speaking, a sea glimpse – a fragment of colour, an occasional glitter amongst the tamarisk and pampas grass – but Flat 1 had its own front door, and a whole façade of windows through which Atlantic light poured in. And it was inextricable from the enchantment of that first holiday, of future holidays: twice a year, until I was well into my teens, with exceptions that I can count on the fingers of one hand.

The fishermen of Port Isaac once plotted the coordinates of their watery grounds as sets of marks that, seen from the spot in question, were visually aligned: 'Tintagel Church Tower touching Otterham or Gull Rock', for example, and 'Mouls Island touching Pentire Head', at the intersection of which sight lines lay good crabbing or lobstering terrain. I chart my way to the cove by my own kind of triangulation between Rough Tor and Rumps Point and the silhouetted church on its high horizon. Whether I am driving or walking, one or another is in view or, if not visible, always there, beyond an incline or a headland: a felt, interior landmark. When I have driven across England and, at a certain point on the A30, Rough Tor materialises in the atmosphere – and later, on the bright coast road, always somehow bright whatever the weather, I glimpse the headland hillfort or the clifftop church, I feel something that I can only describe as overwhelming connection. I am oriented by these landmarks in more than the navigational sense. Their various conjunctions, one to another, bring me to the cove, this place where I am so . . . intensely alive. Where, for all of its strange and dangerous ways, I feel safe within myself.

*

My cove may not evade the digital magnifying glass of Google Maps, but on paper it has a slightly fugitive quality. It haunts the margins of more than a few maps, straddling early Ordnance Survey sheets or falling, as it does in one old guidebook, into the gutter of a two-page spread. In another classic guide, it slips beyond the right-hand edge of a map printed on a recto page; the map continues overleaf but, when you turn the page, you will find yourself beyond the cove.

Then again, coves are by definition enigmatic, marginal places. Their surfaces are seabed and terra firma. They are enclosed, and they are not. You do not go onto a cove as you do a beach, howsoever each is bounded by land and open to the sea: you go into it, as you go into a garden or a room, like the little rooms in which the word 'cove' originated. *Cofa* is an Old English word for an inner chamber or monastic cell, about as close as you can get to a spatial definition of privacy. But those spaces did not remain tightly closed for long; by the time the Normans built the little church up at Tintagel, a *cofa* could be a cave or den, a recess in a rock, and the rest is history. 'Coves' were still bound up with self-containment, yet they had somehow opened up along the way. In a cove you might be private, secluded – safe – and at the same time see, hear, smell, be connected with what lies beyond. A cove is a beautiful paradox. It is the best of both worlds, like a good corner.

I like a good corner. There was a time when I did not think about corners at all, but at a certain point in my childhood I began not just to appreciate them, but to seek them out. In cafés, pubs, waiting rooms, departure lounges a part of me is on high alert if I cannot sit against a wall, and ideally in an angle formed by two. If someone is behind my back – walking past, or doing something or simply being there – I do not feel safe. I am blessed with an endlessly kind husband who chooses his battles in public places and, for good measure, always takes the aisle seat.

The beautiful paradox of the coastal cove is nevertheless a dangerous one. It is hospitable to the human scale, a place of shelter from the weather and the open sea, yet it gives onto and intermingles with that elemental world: its depths and infinitude, its sheer brute impersonal force. Your place of shelter can be one of peril. Should you hide yourself away too comfortably in your intertidal recess you might find yourself in trouble on rocks, or drown; be cornered, as it were.

When I say that I have known the cove for my entire life, I am not as sure as I used to be what I mean by that. For years I thought I knew the place like the back of my hand. There were exceptions, naturally, like the dark caves on the sunless side, and the fact that no place stays the same for long, least of all a coastal one; bits of cliff crumbled and rocks fell and configurations of water and shingle changed from one season to the next. Yet, when all was said and done, it was my cove. I knew my way around its rocks and crevices, its registers of sound and smell, and I knew it in that visceral way of knowing a place, however uninhabitable: the feeling, when you've stepped down with the stream and tread on that shingle, taste seaweed on the air, a special echo in your ears, that you are back.

I take it as read that nostalgia is woven into my relationship with this place; it couldn't not be given that I came here in childhood, on holiday and at a time when my parents were alive. Yet even when I was very small, way too young to try to conceptualise such things, I had a feeling about the cove that I didn't have about other places, other coves even, that I loved.

When I was there, it was exactly where I wanted to be: I felt that I was living to the outermost reaches of my senses, and I felt something that even now I cannot quite put into words, a kind of wonder that had no specific object but was rather a way of being. Once I was old enough to experience the world and time in more than immediate terms, the cove began to call me back when I was not there. It made itself a point of reference in my being: an enduring connection too complex and intense to be filed under happy holidays.

I am over fifty now, but no more able to pinpoint that feeling of connection than was my childhood self who knew the place inside out unquestioningly. It has evolved and morphed, this compulsion to return. Like a phantom thing it eludes me the more I try to grasp it and look at it closely, and ask questions of it. Maybe you can know a place too well, in your own way, and one day some unexpected happening, some new development, will show you that, actually, you don't know it very well at all.

Maybe this place will turn the tables and start asking questions of you. Who on earth you think you are, with your assumptions and presumptions. Whether you are sure that you feel no fear – not the tiniest flicker – when you pick your way down through the slippery gulley or jump your way across the cove, one rock to the next. Whether you really, hand on heart, one-hundred-and-seventeen per cent don't believe in ghosts. Depending, of course, on what you mean by 'ghost'.

*

On the last Friday of school at Easter or the October half-term, my father came home from work and loaded the car and drove us across the foot of England into the night. East Sussex – West Sussex – Hampshire – Wiltshire – Dorset – Somerset – Dorset again – Devon – Cornwall: I knew the route west like the order of the planets and the colours of the rainbow. I did not care to learn it in the opposite direction, for I dreaded leaving Cornwall. On the journey home, east, I felt something that was more than sadness, a special grief; I do still. I wanted the road skimming Bodmin moor to go on forever; I willed Rough Tor to stay there to the right, close enough to touch or far away depending on the weather.

My parents worked hard in every sense for these holidays. I wish I could say I did not take it for granted at the time, as I suppose children cannot but do. It puts me to shame today to think how, working full-time, my mother shopped and cooked and baked to feed everyone for a week and sometimes two – the only exception was shop bread towards the end of the holiday – and how she organised bedding and towels, for self-catering meant self-catering, and clothes, hot-water bottles, a sharp breadknife, hard-negotiated quotas of toys, and piled everything up with the boxes of food inside the front door. How my father, home in good time and following a routine protestation to the effect that it would never all fit in, nevertheless fitted all of it, all of us and the flatulent Treacle, into the Cortina – and how he set off on that long, long drive at the lowest ebb of his working week. The overnight journey was set in stone, for we gained thereby a whole precious day on cliffs or beaches, or down in coves, down in the cove. My mother had an arrangement with Mrs Harris, and the key was left under a lump of slate on the top step. On a good run with sleepy children the journey took just over eight hours, for the M25 was barely under construction and our way threaded through places with special names like Piltdown and Wincanton, Ottery St Mary, Sticklepath. We turned left at the garden gate and drove down the lane, due west for Cornwall. For the first few minutes there was a guessing game as to what my mother might have forgotten to pack; once we had reached the end of the lane there was no more guessing and no going back, not even for my mother's address book. Hot-water bottles, I said once as the car was slowing, the indicator clicking, and my mother sighed and my father turned the car and we went home and headed off again, left at the garden gate, down the lane, due west to Cornwall.

We pulled up quietly in the middle of the night like people in a film, the headlights off, gravel crunching significantly as my father rode the clutch. I remember arriving in another world, a steady salt wind and nothing but dark, pure dark all the way, not that I knew it then, to Newfoundland. *Dark is kind*: at a certain point in my childhood I read and reread Jill Tomlinson's story about Plop the anxious owl until my Puffin paperback fell apart. *Dark is exciting – necessary – beautiful –* and nowhere was it more so than in this place at a mysterious hour through which I slept in everyday life. One day I would learn just how complicated a time for body and soul this is – that, within the infinite space between roughly one and three, minds unravel and dimensions unfold – but I felt then its strangeness and its power.

While my parents unpacked the car in a silent operation, I headed up the high slate steps and tiptoed from room to room to check that everything was still in place – the glittery plastic door handles, the brown vinyl three-piece suite, the miniature drawer in the dressing table that was mine alone for the next week, or two, and in which I would squirrel precious findings away. The washbasin in the corner of the bedroom, the special thud of linoleum and its static stickiness to my socks. The composite smell of salt and sand and something innate that, were we not on holiday, might have been a touch unpleasant, stale. In the morning, whatever the weather and however short the night, my mother would make sandwiches and we'd drive back around the Camel Estuary and take first the coast road and then ever-narrowing lanes – the high hedgebanks, the glimpses of sea – and we'd park at Tregardock and I'd check on the pigs, and then we would set off on foot for the cove. It was inconceivable to my mother that we would spend the first day of our holiday anywhere else.

It is not uncommon for a place where you have spent childhood holidays to become a place in your grown-up heart. Maybe you have not been back for years, decades even, and that yen for Sidmouth or St Ives is not for somewhere you would recognise today, but for a place shaped by feeling and memory. Or perhaps it is hardwired into your family, like Christmas traditions or home itself, and you simply never stopped going back; you are middle-aged now, and may or may not have children of your own in tow. Retrospect makes ideal times of holidays, but then again holidays often are ideal in real time. They are anticipated, dreamed of, and above all wrapped in special dispensation. Holidays are just that – holidays, holy days, days of leave from the everyday – and this may make you more than usually inclined to find your expectations fulfilled. I could not compute that the Harrises actually lived in the flat above: they must surely, as we were when we were here, be exempt from the obligations of real life, and I was astonished when their boys passed the window one morning wearing blazers and ties. Were the Harrises really going to school? I asked my mother. And did this mean that they watched television *every day*? Theme tunes travelled down through the ceiling; I had my suspicions.

Each of these biannual trips was a feast of magical exceptions to our own everyday. For starters there was, as there wasn't at home, a television. My father bought, and we fell upon, the *Radio* and *TV Times*. By today's standards the choice was limited, for one of the three channels appeared to offer educational stuff and Test Card F (the one with the hairband and Bubbles the Clown), but our viewing was researched and debated very seriously indeed. There were unwholesome treats: cream of tomato soup in Thermos flasks, extra cake for the long walk back, shop bread (though never, ever white) towards the end of the second Easter week. Chocolate-chip cookies and ginger nuts in the baking of which I had a progressively autonomous hand; the cookery book in question now sits on the bookshelf in my own kitchen. Page 158 is encrusted with forty-five-year-old dough, and a congealed blob of Muscovado sugar has burned a hole in the accompanying photograph; for what it's worth, a porridge oat from an unrelated project is embedded in the method for ginger nuts. There was soft, soft water that lathered in the bath and, when I was old enough to appreciate such things, made a perfect cup of tea. Evenings were spent gathered around the television in sleeping bags with hot-water bottles; only decades later would it occur to me that this cosy holiday tradition was born of conditions that paying guests would not countenance today. In between our carefully chosen programmes we watched anything, and everything. I loved the adverts on ITV.

And there was Fry's Turkish Delight, jewel-coloured inside and out, its glistening wrapper folded and tucked like an envelope: we were allowed to choose a bar of chocolate every day for our evening treat, something that happened only on Saturdays at home. More often than not this daily errand was run in Pendoggett, a village that, were it not for the Post Office store, I would have loved for its name alone. The little shop, now long gone, was neatly crammed with things like Lux soap, Camp coffee, luggage labels with looped fawn string, china ornaments, all presided over by an elderly man in a proper shopkeeper's dustcoat. Once I spent some of my own money on a bar of Lux, as advertised that week on ITV: it seemed so exotic, so, well, luxurious, and I remember that the old man seemed quietly amused at the apparent enormity of my purchase. I agonised long and hard over the ranged confectionery but always ended up with Turkish Delight; the colour was to die for, beyond rosiness, and there was something sumptuous about the way the chocolate coating cracked and imploded with each bite.

One of the myriad reasons for going on holiday was to spend your hard-saved pocket money. There was the shop selling rocks and minerals with lovely names like feldspar and tourmaline, amethyst the very meaning of purple. The newsagent with a marvellous stand of Tor Mark booklets about Cornish place names, seashells, words, folklore, flowers: I budgeted and collected them one by one. The surf shop where I almost always invested in a multiheaded windmill that was like a whirring rainbow. The toy shop where we bought practical jokes like Snappy Gum and Nail Thru' Finger and, my favourite, a fairly convincing plastic fried egg. Early one morning I crept out and placed it on the bonnet of the car, and my father rose to the occasion magnificently. I loved the old-school chemist because it smelled of Yardleys; I purchased a pink tin of cherry-flavoured cough sweets there, though I was perfectly well. I even splashed out on a tabloid newspaper once, because I could. I'd no intention of reading it, but buying a paper seemed like a grown-up, independent thing to do. I did open and close the paper repeatedly, which is what adults did when they read newspapers – that this was how you turned the pages of a broadsheet had not yet dawned on me – and noticed, to my indignation, that Page 3 was missing. I think my mother had something to do with that.

But above all, even above the shopping and television, the Turkish Delight, there was the sea. The sea air, the sea sound, the sea light, the being there. I cannot recall a time when I did not long for these things. I felt a surge of happiness, wide awake in the back seat between my sleeping siblings, as we crossed the Tamar into Cornwall: 'KERNOW'. I would ask my father to open the car window, for though there were miles yet to go I was sure that I could smell the sea. These days I open the window myself, but my heart feels the same fullness when I see that county sign. It means that tomorrow I will go to the cove.

Down the farm track past the pigsty, the streams and high hedgebanks, the navelworts, the ferns and overarching thorns. A mingled smell of damp green, damp slate and herbiverous dung. Through the rotten kissing gate, its slate enclosure as old as the hills, over a patch of perpetual squelchiness. Out onto a bright green field and there's the sea, its colour and its gravelly resonance. Down amongst blackthorns, musky in spring and foaming like the waves themselves. The sea echo gone now, cut off by a bracken-covered crag across the valley end. You could, should you wish, walk around The Mountain and continue down to the beach, but you do not. You turn north up the valley side, a bright climb through gorse and heather. A stile onto the open clifftop – you pause, winded by the force of the air, and look back. The high cliffs and their tumbled chaos all the way to Rumps Point, Puffin Island. The beach below, monochrome, sea spray drifting in with the waves, the dark-bright sand, the black rocks mysterious in brilliant haze. The surf in which, I learned many years after the event, a little boy was dragged to his death. He was nine years old, my age exactly.

On along the cliff path, thrift and thyme and green-white drifts of wild carrot. *Tregardock Treligga Trebarwith Treknow:* your footsteps keep time with the names of the place. The hedge-banks of slate and vegetation. The church ahead on its empty horizon, neither distant nor proximate, coming and going with the rise of the ground. The bit of path that seems closer to the edge each time you tread it, and probably is. Past the tower in its flat green field. Across the crumbly corner where the rabbit holes are. Over the common: the earthworks, the gorse, the concrete bunker off to the right. Ruby-red cows. On to the high headland and the tumuli, a spot that feels otherworldly because it is absolutely exposed, owned by the Atlantic: its beauty and its brunt. The church right there, all at once, miles of intervening topography elided by the valley brow. Any minute now you will look down on the cove. Its rocky confines may contain heaving sea, or hurl the waves back in some crashing melodrama. Maybe the tide is low and the cove crammed with slate: sloping bedrock and sea-smoothed boulders, and formations vaguely resembling a boot and a snail that has lost or retracted its tentacles. The scene below, whichever it may be, is vivid and distant as if seen through inverted binoculars, or dreamed.

Deep down into the valley. Tracks and gouges and slaty

ruins, turbulent ground. The sliced cliff face. At some point, unless it is very, very wet, you will leave the zigzagging path and step straight down with a dizzy thrill, the slope falling to the stream. Along an edge of overhanging thrift and grass – quickly, lightly, don't stop now. Into the gulley cut through slate, its sheer façades and, underfoot, vaguely geometric planes that suggest steps but are nothing of the kind: they pitch you downwards and are slimy with moisture and algae, and some kind of sediment. You feel for footholds that are not quite there, reach out for the sunless wall to your left – it drips and runs, transpiring or perspiring – though there is nothing to grasp but navelworts and miniature maritime ferns. That it might be dangerous has never occurred to you, for your father could not fall and nor, therefore, can you. The gulley conducts you as through a portal into the light, into the cove.

I have longed to be here and here I am. I never know where to start. I want to take it all in at once and I want to linger in every detail, one stone or gust, one sprig of seaweed at a time. The rusted ring in the cliff face. I clamber onto a lump of quartz like an island in the watery slaty shingle, and look out over the jam-packed rocks, out to sea. The horizon could be a line in a colouring book, either side filled in solidly with felt-tipped pens, the deep-blue sea and the sky-blue sky. The tide is going out.

The shriek of a gull, its reverberating clang. Sounds are bounced and amplified by the enclosing cliffs, the cove an echo chamber. This can be fun, when you are small; you shout a word or two and hear your voice travel around the place, or you engage someone in round after round of colliding ululations. Today, in middle age, the acoustics make me faintly self-conscious. I cough, and when the cough reverberates it is as if the cove is listening to me.

One day, standing on this very rock, I will narrowly escape death. For now, though, there is the cave to check on: it is shallow and light, a place in which to eat sandwiches on rainy days, and because the tide leaves things behind – snagged knots of seaweed and nylon net, a jellyfish blob, a herring gull corpse – it has a perennial air of fishiness. Here, absorbed to a drying rock like a fossilised fern that photosynthesised 320 million years ago, is an impossibly delicate fragment of weed: I prise it away with a thumbnail and tuck it into my notebook. Here is the rock of smoothed slate into which mysterious rings are scored, neither wholly circular nor yet quite elliptical. And the clean-edged rhomboid one, strangely regular amongst the rest; when the sun moves around the dark surface will gleam like bronze. There is the cove to cross, one wet weed-covered rock to another, the widening stream and the sloshing tide, little slates wedged in between like After Eight mints in opened boxes; black mussels and crustaceous barnacles. One giant leap at a time, deeper and deeper into the cove.

The sea-blue, sea-green waves ahead, high in my field of vision: their perpetual advance and mysterious restraint. I wonder why people speak of looking out to sea when I almost always feel myself to be looking up at it. The rock on which I have come to rest is fringed with some kind of brownish wrack. Sea still washes over it, and the weed trails out with the push of each wave like something blossoming.

The precipitous cliff, its sheer oblong faces, the valley climbing up above, slate below sloping like lava. What is not of sea here is, to all appearances, of slate. The snail, of course, and the boot-shaped rock where cormorants congregate; three are lined up along the top, their wings outspread, looking out to sea in an attitude of absolute attentiveness. The pillar: it is roughly cuboid and stands proud of the cliff, forming a frame within which moments of the cove's life are enacted. In one scene a wave breaks over a rock. In another the high tide heaves, or a slice of cliff is dotted with nesting gulls on ledges like tenements, or there is sky. The cliff face is vibrant on this sunshiny day, all the shades of bronze through pewter. When I look up the brilliance burns my eyes. The high grassed edges, the pale marly layer like marzipan on Christmas cake: the world spread thinly over slate.

I'm scrambling now, across the slope. The outgoing tide has left the slate slick. Small worlds of sea will be contained in the dips and crevices, some pink with paintweed, every one of them harbouring mysterious life. Minute seaweeds spaced just so, as if a gardener had planted them there, in clumps and groves, shifting and spreading when the water shifts infinitesimally. Gelatinous anemones in bloom, limpets and mustard-coloured periwinkles: this place could make a child of you. I squat down on the slippery slate, balancing on the balls of my feet, and peer into the first lucid pool.

*

Lights out. The expectant whir of the projector fan. Dust motes dynamic in the brilliant beam. A blank frame: the white wall, its distinctive grain. A shadow hand. And another, someone doing bunny ears. A hot metallic smell. *Ker-chunk*, the first slide clicking into view. And another one. We are in the mid-seventies.

A tremendous sense of occasion surrounded the family slide

show, what with the living room rearranged and blacked out like a cinema. For my father it was a rather more prosaic business, often entailing a torchlit search for the long extension cable in one of the sheds; the unearthing and setting-up of the projector; the slide-by-slide loading of the magazine; and not uncommonly, for like Christmas tree lights the projector did not take kindly to being switched on, an eleventh-hour operation to replace the bulb. My father stockpiled little bulbs. When the dark evenings came around I often badgered my parents to get the slides out, and once in a while they gave in. We didn't have a television after all.

I also loved the slide shows because they told me, in Agfa-chrome colour, a version of my story. The transparencies span roughly the first decade of my life between the black-and-white record of my family's earliest years and my father's transition to colour negative film around the time that, aged eleven, I acquired a camera of my own. Like the monochrome prints of my immediate prehistory the slides are a finite number, for my parents did not have money to spare and the cost of film and processing was material. It made you consider every shot, whether to take it at all and, if you did, your decisions about aperture versus shutter speed, and composition; it made you mindful. Even though the later slides recorded moments that were relatively recent they made me conscious, for all of my inconsiderable years, of having a past – an impression no doubt reinforced by the shows' infrequency. There were things I remembered and things I may have thought I remembered because I was there, and always some new nugget or other: explanations and, especially, dropped comments. I picked those up and stored them away with care:

. . . You loved that coat, didn't you? Remember how
hard we saved for it? . . .

. . . said it was the Big C . . .

. . . I was just about expecting . . .

. . . Poor Bill. That was before . . . silly man. Awful
woman . . . Shhh . . . Which awful woman, Mummy?
Um – oh – Auntie— Oh look, there you are in your
carrycot! We left it behind once, with you in it. In the
hall, fast asleep. We were going to Tunbridge Wells to
buy school shoes, the others were so excited, and we got
right to the end of the lane and Daddy said do we have
Beth with us? My heart was in my mouth all the way
back up the hill, but there you were, still sound asleep,
no harm done . . .

Ker-chunk. A family picnic on the South Downs, my mother
in a gorgeous lime-green shift dress (yes of course I made it
myself), pouring coffee from a tartan Thermos that I've never
seen in real life. *Ker-chunk*. My siblings in winter coats and hats,
hand in hand. *Ker-chunk*. Treacle in front of the herbaceous
border, Japanese anemones blooming pink. *Ker-chunk*. My
mother perched on a rock, looking out to sea, an open novel
face-down on her knee. *Ker-chunk*. And here I am in the cove
aged about four, squatting on that slippery slope. The slate
beneath my feet is gleaming wet, but just above me the slope
is dry; the tide must be going out in the photograph too. The
day is dull, the sky a little overexposed. I am wearing a brown
hooded sweater that my grandmother knitted to last, my siblings having worn it in turn before it was handed down to me.
The wool is coarse and a little scratchy, not that you'd know it

from the photograph, and in damp weather a coating of mist collects on the wispy fibres and the sweater smells more strongly than ever of wool. I'm leaning forward in my shiny wellingtons, reaching down the slippery incline with a seaside-issue fishing net, captivated by the rock pool below. I am invincible, defying gravity, though the tension generated by my downward force has made my sweater ride up to reveal a white T-shirt stretched across a small pot belly. I've no idea that, as the photograph records, my father is balanced on the dry rock behind me, holding my hood. It is not so much that I know I cannot fall, rather that the possibility of falling does not occur to me.

*

Rock is the enduring stuff of biblical metaphor, and it is mutable. It comes into being by stratification, lithification, metamorphosis (I love those words). It shifts and it melts; sometimes it erupts. Alpine peaks and cliffs and pebbles have their being in a condition of perpetual weathering, washing, churning. The sleek surface of a marble statue grows granulated, sugary; a headstone fades from legibility. A piece of slate grows wave-shaped with the waves. The wearing and loosening forces of nature may be enmeshed with human ones in this world of acid rain and toxic encrustation, weather driven to extremes, sea levels rising; even so, the rate at which rock erodes is mostly to the geological side of time, imperceptible from one minute or day to the next. Quarrymen, on the other hand, shape rocky places in real time. The man in this grainy black-and-white image is doing just that.

To say that the man is standing does not quite correlate with what is beneath his feet. He is on or at a cliff face – a preposition-defying place, no place for a person – and his back is turned to planes of slate that tilt slightly as though Cézanne had painted them. He is facing the Atlantic, though he does not have the luxury of contemplating its immensity. His feet, squarely apart, span a ledge that is not really a ledge so much as a sliver; the toes of his hobnailed boots project into nothing. Below, out of our view but not the man's – far from it – ocean collides with land. This is a place for seabirds, and even gulls do not perch easily on the edges and irregularities of a rockface like this. They adjust their balance, one scaly foot to the other, swaying slightly.

The man wears a flat cap, corduroy trousers and a moleskin waistcoat, labourer's clothes; his billowing shirt sleeves are tied in at the wrists. A length of rope falling from above is looped about his waist and back over one shoulder. He must be secure or inured to danger, for his posture belongs to another context: somewhere firm and open, like a field. The man is not balancing nor perching on that unlikely edge, nor paralysed with terror – at least, not visibly – but standing with a sledgehammer raised in one hand. His other hand steadies a metal pole positioned in the cliff face, and he is about to swing the sledgehammer across his body to whack the jumper, as the chisel-tipped pole is called, further into the rock. He has been doing this for his entire shift, maybe with a partner, maybe not, rotating the jumper by half a turn with each blow: the action of drilling reduced to its constituent parts, parsed in laborious slow motion. It takes the best part of a working day to bore a hole six feet deep by this method. The pneumatic drill has been transformative in many British quarries, but modern technology is costly and in any case the days of this cliff quarry are numbered. Additional holes will be drilled at strategic intervals, packed with gunpowder and detonated. The loosened blocks, upwards of two tons in weight, will be levered out and secured with chains – I cannot visualise how this might be achieved by men working effectively in thin air – and winched to the clifftop where they will be cut and split and trimmed or 'dressed' into roofing slates. The quarryman's face is obscured by the peak of his cap as he concentrates on his aim. It could be the early 1890s; let's say 1891, a census year.

The quarryman might have walked to work over fields, or along the cliff path from Trevena, as the village of Tintagel was named at the time, or from any one of the surrounding settlements. Maybe he came from Trebarwith, a hamlet just inland from Trebarwith Strand, his hobnails grating and clanging down the stony track, the rising slate. There are fewer quarrymen in Trebarwith than there used to be. Of sixteen heads of household entered in the 1841 census, ten were quarrymen; fifty years later the hamlet's recorded population has dropped to nine households, with just three quarrymen amongst their heads. Coastal slate quarrying is on the wane. By the turn of the century much of the infrastructure will have been dismantled and repurposed elsewhere, structures stripped of roofing slates and usable stone, their remnants left to the weather and whatever lives and grows in this place. Long Grass, the last commercial quarry on these cliffs, will cease operating in 1937 following a fatal accident.

Why, when there was excellent slate to be found inland around Delabole, would the lives of men in a dangerous industry be jeopardised further in order to extract slate at cliff faces? Slate is a type of metamorphic rock, mudstone altered under heat and pressure generated by stirrings in the earth's crust. Subterranean slate, like the solid stone quarried up at Delabole, is formed under high metamorphic pressure. Because coastal slate – slate in outcrop – has metamorphosed under lower pressure, its structural properties are different and uniquely valuable. Slate in outcrop is jointed: it has natural fracture lines that lend it to extraction in smaller, more manageable blocks. Outcrop formations of slate, moreover, are commonly foliated like the leaves of a book, readily split along their flat planes into thin, hard sheets or laminae. All in all, nature could not have designed a more serviceable roofing material; the early modern topographer John Norden declared Cornish slate 'the beste . . . to cover howses' because the split and finished slates are 'thynn, beautyfull, and lighte', and, unless they meet with some kind of 'violence', extremely durable.

The cliffs along this stretch of coast were formed from a variety of mudstones on diverse tectonic occasions tens, hundreds of millions of years apart, making for rock that is richly variable within small areas. When these slates are good they are very good indeed, and when they are bad they are useless. The cliffs were drilled and blasted, hacked, shovelled away over centuries, and when quarrymen hit upon inferior slate they worked around it and carried on, leaving behind scullocks, as these dramatic lumps are known in quarrying parlance. The pillar that Tennyson saw on his walk and the cuboid column down in the cove are both scullocks, sculpted by accident. Scullocks sometimes look like sculptures but are the antithesis thereof. A sculptor shapes a block of stone by chipping waste away; a scullock, on the other hand, is the very shape of waste.

The image of the quarryman is reproduced on the cover of an archaeological report; I came across it not so long ago when reading around the sparsely documented history of coastal slate quarrying. I suspect the photograph was posed in an accessible spot, given that the telephoto lens was a recent and very costly invention. In a way this necessary artifice makes the image all the more compelling, for the actual working conditions of the hammer-drilling man are too dangerous for us to see for ourselves. We must use our imaginations to port the standing man to an interface of rock and wind and sea, a world resolved into elements.

That elemental world sounds sublime, but is not. The quarryman has no choice, as I have, in returning to these cliffs. Maybe he is forty-three years old, like one of the few quarryman who lived in Trebarwith in 1891, but his occupation has given him the body of a much older man. All that scaling of rockfaces and balancing, manoeuvring, repetitive hammering: the physical graft that kept him fit for a youthful interval has wrecked his joints and nerve endings. It has taken its toll on his nerves in other ways, too; you may convince yourself that you've a stomach for heights, for risking your life in your daily work – you have to – but that is not the same as knowing or feeling a thing to be true. Not to mention his lungs; the open air in which he works is hardly the tonic saltiness that I inhale here today. There is smoke from sheds and crib huts, smithies and so on. Sulphurous fallout from detonated rock. Dust from drilling, dust from cutting, dust from splitting; silicosis, a lung disease caused by exposure to particles of stone, is not confined to those who mine slate underground. The first Workmen's Compensation Act will not be passed for another six years, and even then its scope will not extend to industrial disease. And the lively moods of Atlantic weather are far from inspiring when you are exposed to them every working day. You can get soaked and frozen here at any time of year and, in summer, scorched. The winds make rain wetter and colder, the burning sun harsher, the work at the rockface more difficult and dangerous. And how you are ageing can become irrelevant in an instant. All it takes is a misplaced step or a rope secured too hastily, or maybe a two-ton block of slate slipping from its chains, like the one that will smash a man off the cliff at Long Grass in 1936. Death is never very far away. You get used to living on the edge.

According to the 1891 census return, our Trebarwith quarryman has a six-year-old daughter. She has an occupation of her own: she is a 'scholar', one who goes to school. I'm sure she roams around the valley and up to the headland above the cove. Gulls and buzzards glide at her feet. The tumuli and the echoing sea. The common is just that, common land; the donkeys graze up here when they are not carting slate or sand. Beyond there is no sign of a red-brick tower, nor for that matter a level green expanse, but a reticulation of ancient hedgebanks and sloping fields with names like Best Park, Lower Field, Middle Field, Long Willies.

I wonder if the little girl has watched a starfish feel its way around a low-tide pool, or held a quartz pebble in the palm of her hand. Its special white heaviness.

Maybe, one day, she will see a rainbow here.

*

Danger is latent in this elemental interface: all it needs is a human protagonist. The ocean's 'grand violence' at the cliffs around Tintagel inspired the Victorian novelist Anthony Trollope (from a safe remove, of course) to write a short story, 'Malachi's Cove', at the heart of which is a dramatic near-drowning amid deadly rocks and a fast-rising tide. Not to mention the cliff a little further north, near Boscastle, that gave English literature arguably its most significant edge since the scene at Dover in *King Lear*. Before its first publication in book form in 1873, Thomas Hardy's Cornish novel *A Pair of Blue Eyes* was serialised in *Tinsleys' Magazine*. The instalment for February 1873 escalates when Henry Knight, a rival for the affections of the feisty heroine Elfride Swancourt, loses his hat in a gust of wind and, chasing after it, slips over the edge of a cliff. And what a cliff: a 'precipice', a 'shaly' and 'treacherous incline', 'sheer perpendicularity' above a 'nether sky', the sky-reflecting sea. A scene of high drama ensues, in the course of which Elfride tries to help Knight and slips down the incline herself; is able to clamber to safety while her self-sacrificing suitor falls further; establishes that there is no sign of anyone who might come to their aid; and, with barely ten minutes' strength remaining in Knight's hands, vanishes. At the close of the instalment Knight is 'literally suspended by his arms', hanging from the cliff edge, feeling himself 'in the presence of a personalized loneliness'. Readers will have to wait an entire month to discover whether he survives or falls to his death (spoiler: he is rescued, with a rope knotted from Elfride's hastily removed underwear). This is widely held to be the origin of the term 'cliffhanger', the sine qua non of modern serial broadcasting as of Victorian serial fiction: it kept readers buying and reading as it keeps soap audiences tuning in. Like the hapless Knight, Hardy's reader is left in suspense, albeit of a safe and thrilling kind, thoroughly motivated to stump up a shilling for the March issue of *Tinsleys'*.

But the lived dramas of the North Cornwall coast are starkly unromantic and the opposite of thrilling. Ships have foundered time and again on submerged rocks just offshore; their wrecks plot a kind of ghost coastline on the seabed. Who knows how many fishermen's lives have been claimed by the same rocks and rough seas over centuries, millennia. Quarrymen have fallen to their deaths from cliffs. And on beaches in the neighbourhood of the cove people have been washed off rocks while harvesting seaweed and shellfish, or fishing with rods, or engaged in recreational daredevilry, leaning over to photograph something, scattering ashes. Holidays have flipped into tragedy through innocence of what the sea can do, or sheer bad luck. Think of the boy who drowned at Tregardock when we both were nine: a rip current dragged him under as he jumped waves close to the shore. Decades later his brother, Richard Beard, pieced together the events of *The Day That Went Missing* (as the title of his harrowing memoir goes). I remember chancing upon a copy in a London bookshop, the recognition and the horror. Tregardock was one of our places too, and from the author's painful returnings in memory and on the ground I have a fairly clear idea of the spot on which his little brother lost his life.

When I think today about some of the places my family frequented in North Cornwall I have a strong impression, as I didn't at the time, of intrepidity. More than that, it bemuses me that my memories of the holidays we spent there are untouched by any consciousness of physical danger. I certainly knew what fear felt like. Balls frightened me because they often hit me on the head. I knew terror too, just the once, when I was very small and one of my siblings crept into my bedroom wearing a teddy-bear mask. It was a ghastly thing, run up from an old blanket and pulled on right over the head. I was almost asleep on a light summer evening and the mask had round holes where eyes and mouth ought to be, and I glimpsed something moving, flickering inside, and the monstrous head belonged to a human body.

Yet I do not recall ever feeling unsafe as I stepped down through the trickling, darkly tilting gulley, or hurried along a narrow path to look out to sea from my favourite ledge. I was certainly careful, and I knew that I was not to visit the ruined wreckers' cottage unaccompanied – but when we leapt our way across the cove, I paid no attention to the gaps between the rocks, to the possibility that I might miss my footing and smash an elbow, sprain something. It was par for the course, such was the preciousness of every last low-tide minute, to make a dash, to scramble or wade back around the foot of the cliff because the waves were suddenly there. I watched with equanimity when my father climbed some way down a grassy-glossy cliff to help a panicking lamb. I remember looking at the rocks below, the seething dark water, but because my father was my father everything would be alright.

Maybe there was no danger so long as you trod carefully; maybe there was, and I was oblivious. This was, after all, a child who liked to canter on ponies along the verges of Sussex roads, jumping one drainage ditch after another – until someone tipped her parents off and they went berserk. My parents were not reckless people. If they took a certain route down a cliff, or allowed us to roam off into further reaches of coves, I knew that it was safe to do so. Yet friends of mine who are now parents would be aghast to imagine their own children busy on some of those edges and ledges, vanishing into some recess or other. It is true that I grew up in the countryside in times to which, for better or worse, the idea of risk assessment had not occurred – when, by way of a junior geography lesson, my class was once turned loose in the woods: we spent the morning messing around before making our own way back to school, down the lane in drips and drabs, in our collective own good time, and that everyone returned safely for lunch, that nobody encountered a stranger nor fell into one of the old ironworks streams was nothing more than bloody good luck. You climbed down *there*? said my husband Shaun when, years later, I showed him the way down to Beacon Cove, another old haunt. Of course we did, I said, until the cliff fell away.

At home in Sussex I would take myself off to Cornwall in my thoughts. It was a place where I felt more than happy – where I felt that I was myself. *Tregardock Treligga Trebarwith Treknow*: I thought my way along paths and over beaches, wet sand beneath my feet, its solid thud, the wind and the gulls. The Atlantic thundering. Down cliffs and into coves – into my cove, of course, and the valley's abandoned intricacies. The seaweed smell, the sea-sky light, everything singing. Lemon cake. Cream of tomato soup. As my mother began to make lists and checked that our waterproofs still fitted, and my father talked about servicing the car, and we all started collecting coins for the flat's voracious electricity meter, a happy impatience possessed me. Four weeks and one night, two weeks exactly, three nights, tomorrow!

But at some point in my childhood complications arose. Every evening in those last two weeks (fourteen nights exactly, three, tomorrow!), tucked up in bed, my thoughts trod the same paths, made the same circuits of beaches and coves – and as they did so excitement darkened to its flip side, dread. I was seven or eight and had begun to suffer from bedtime angst. It had its own soundtrack, a song that I heard one autumn evening: it was dark outside and snug indoors, and my siblings were listening to pop songs on the radio – something that made me feel vicariously worldly. I adored ABBA and knew the words to Johnny Nash's 'I Can See Clearly Now', albeit the incidence of 'bright' appeared to change every time the song was played. On the evening in question, however, I heard Terry Jacks pick out the first notes of 'Seasons in the Sun'. The song had been around for a year or two, in the warp and weft of things, but I'd never really listened to it. Now, feeling their way between minor and major, monotone and melody, those twelve world-weary notes shocked me: they still upset me today. I did not understand the lyrics back then, nor know that the song originated in 'Le Moribond' or 'The Dying Man' by Jacques Brel; I didn't need to. *Goodbye my friend, it's hard to die*: the line made something new and terrible turn in my stomach. That, and the word BUT: *We had joy, we had fun, we had seasons in the sun, / But the hills that we climbed were just seasons out of time*. Whatever seasons out of time were; they sounded lofty, and at odds with the way of things. I'd found more worldliness than I had bargained for. Whether this terrible discovery was a single event on that vivid Sunday evening – the dusky lampshades, the lovely fire, the sitting room suddenly not quite safe – or whether the song gave shape to something that was already in the air, something to do with growing up, I ceased to sleep soundly. I was perfectly fine throughout the day if often tired, but as soon as my parents had said good night and closed my bedroom door my thoughts went looking for trouble; if no immediate subject presented itself they rooted out things from which to manufacture catastrophe. The cliffs and tides of North Cornwall, the places that I loved, were perfect material.

I visualised a sandy cove that had its own special shells; they were whitish and patterned with wavy brown lines. The main part of the cove offered little fodder for worry, for it was accessed by a margin of sand that remained above the high-tide line – but we frequented parts that only became accessible as the waves receded. We could get cut off there! And there! And the bit around the corner where we lit campfires and there were oystercatchers: would we be able to scramble up the cliff if the tide should catch us unawares? I didn't think so. There was the descent into Beacon Cove, that precarious path around the hole: what if, one day, it should just . . . collapse? And then, assuming we made it around the hole, there was the ledge along which you must tread very carefully, one foot in front of the other, high above the rocks. Surely we would not go to Beacon Cove again: something was going to happen there! My imagination spun off to a narrow stretch of the cliff path on the way to Rumps Point, where gorse bloomed golden on one side and, on the other, far below, the sea was an impossible shade of blue: as I lay awake in Sussex, my busy brain connected the exhilarating path with a blank, vertical edge of land that I glimpsed once as we walked from the opposite direction. If you lost your balance there you would, the sea's lovely colour notwithstanding, drop directly to your death. I moved on to sandy beaches and found danger at their rocky ends. What if we misjudged the tide? What if those tumbled rocks were to tumble further?

Now that I came to think about the cove it terrified me. There were deadly drops and loose edges everywhere. The way down through the gulley was slippery at the best of times: there was nothing for your fingers or feet to grip, and the walls that I now saw in my mind's eye had shaded from their slaty colours to black. Once you were down in the cove itself there was no end of rocks from which to slip and places in which to get cut off. As for the little cove within the cove around the furthest corner, that did not bear thinking about. And what if a lump of slate were to drop from that overhanging cliff edge and you should happen to be in the wrong place at the wrong time? You would die. We were going to the cove in eight days' time: I knew that something terrible was going to happen. By now I was struggling to breathe, gasping for air, and this was heard as noisy sobbing. What on earth is the matter? one or other of my parents pleaded for the umpteenth time, you have to tell me. I can't tell you. It's too awful. TELL ME! I don't want to die. I don't want you to die. Don't be a silly billy, my poor mother said. Is everything going to be alright? Of course it is, my mother said under duress, now you really have to go to sleep. But what if I don't ever sleep again? Is everything going to be alright?

If you sleep soundly, you will not fall.

That was over forty years ago. These days the demons get going later, between about one-thirty and three, though I have learned not to look at the clock; it only tells you how little you have slept or how few hours you have left for sleep. But a heart-thumping scene has stayed with me from that time. It is one of those visceral, real dreams that leach into the following day and dig themselves into your consciousness. I am standing in a narrow recess, watching the sea. Walls of black rock tilt in from either side; they glisten horribly. The sky is grey, drizzling. I can smell driftwood smouldering, seaweed roasting, and above the rumble of the sea my mother's voice echoes unintelligibly. The ocean is before me, moving in: it is grey, as the sky is. The foaming waves are stacked on top of one another. I cannot move. And I know that if I could there is no way out.

I never felt a twinge of anxiety, let alone dread, once we were in Cornwall; quite the contrary. Everything changed when we squeezed into the jam-packed car and headed west towards the light. East Sussex – West Sussex – Hampshire – Wiltshire – Dorset – Somerset – Dorset again – Devon – CORNWALL/ KERNOW: that marvellous lightness, that draught of night air surging in through the wound-down window, promising the sea. For the next week, or two, I would make my way down cliffs, trot along those narrow paths and ledges, roast seaweed if my father remembered the matches, scramble up and down and around the cove, absorbed in the moment and the place. At bedtime, while the others watched grown-up programmes like *Starsky and Hutch* or *Columbo*, I settled down to listen to the thudding wind and thought about the tide that had rolled and crashed back into the cove that afternoon. I'd watched it from my ledge when we had packed up our things and retreated up through the gulley: spray splattered in my face, and the sea's pure power awed me and yet, in a way that I could not fathom, made me feel utterly at peace. I felt that peacefulness now, lying in bed just thinking about it. I thought about other things too. The bustling piglets at Tregardock where we parked, or the surge of March sea around my ankles, how it had made my feet go white and thrilled me to the bone. The way gulls had flapped and drifted about over something in the sea, like flakes of half-combusted paper from a bonfire on a windy day. Our plans for tomorrow, and my plans. I would sleep soundly, I wouldn't fall; in fact I did not give falling a thought. I'd get up early as I almost always did, and tiptoe into the kitchen to fetch one ginger nut and one chocolate-chip cookie from their respective green-striped tins. Then, while the world was still in bed, I would head out into the special light and hurry down to the beach, a whole day and the sea ahead. If it was my turn to choose the day's activities there would be sausages for breakfast. We would then drive up to Tregardock and walk to the cove – unless we had just been there today, in which case we would head south and walk to Beacon Cove.

*

The wind is gale force and straight from the sea. I love days like this, when the weather is really happening. Intense sun and downpours chase in from the west, over the cliffs and on inland towards Bodmin Moor. Earlier, as we came out onto the cliff high above Tregardock, the cloud broke apart and everything was bright, the primroses washed, but it was raining up at Tintagel: vertical lines moved in from the sea and passed straight through the dark little church. When it has just rained, or is about to, and the sky is lead but the sun is shining, the emerald fields have special luminosity and sheep are not white, but whitest. One day, when I get a camera of my own (I would love one for my tenth birthday), this will be my favourite light for taking photographs. Sometimes the weather trips over itself and it rains in sunshine. My father calls this a monkey's birthday. I call it rainbow weather.

Maybe, one day, I will see a rainbow here. I'd like that very much.

The gale snatched and gusted at the corner where the cliff grows blurry and there are rabbit holes. I lost my balance once, and my mother put Treacle on the lead. The tower was there, a little way off in its huge flat field. No path leads to or from it so far as I can tell, and instead of windows the building has black holes like a mask. I am terrified of masks because they turn people into bodies with faces that I cannot read – but even so the tower captivates me. It looks as if it ought to be somewhere else, for the houses and farms around here are whitewashed or slate-coloured yet the tower is built of red brick, just like our house back in Sussex. It is about the same height, too. I think it would be the most amazing thing in the world to climb up inside, right up to the top, and see what I could see. The cove, the valley. The sea without end.

I wish the rabbit holes were not so close to the edge; this seems like a dangerous place for a warren. The soil is pale in a reddish way, and very crumbly, and whenever we pass there are fresh scratchings and droppings. What if a rabbit, burrowing, came out at the cliff face? Would it not fall straight into the sea? I asked my father about this once, and he said no, out of the question, the rabbit would definitely stop in time, rabbits are intelligent and sure-footed creatures. I think I believe him though I do not think he really believes himself. The footpath was altered not long ago; it now cuts across the corner of the cliff instead of running around the edge. I can still see traces of the old path in untrodden grass. I want to walk on what is left of it, to be directly above the sea, but I am not allowed. The wind is blowing steadily again, not pausing for breath, and as we cross the common, the heathery part, I stop and lean out above the sea, just a little. I feel the wind holding me up.

I catch up with my father again, and we stride along side by side singing our songs: *I's the b'y that builds the boat* and, to the tune of 'Wandering Star', *I was born under a gooseberry bush.* Now we are at the headland and the tumuli, as my parents call the two slate-lined hollows on the highest point. I do not know what a tumulus is, except that it is ancient and significant. I never quite get around to asking what tumuli were for; I always seem to be left behind, fiddling around, looking, and by the time I catch up with my parents things have moved on. It suffices that this is a special place. It is bright and bare, and the wind is strong, and the ocean is there at my feet. More often than not, when I look out to sea, there is shadowy land at the outermost edges – but when I stand right here, on the rim of the highest tumulus, a line of silver stretches all the way from left to right. This is how I know that the sea is infinite.

There are rabbit droppings in the second, lower hollow, and skid marks and scattered slate where someone or something has slipped. I crouch down inside, almost on my stomach, until I can barely feel the wind and all I can see is the edge of the ground above me, and the sky. When I stand up again a buzzard is hovering at eye level beyond the cliff. What it sees I can only hear, the heaving ocean colliding with slate. A boom. A thud. A terrible crack. Surf raining down, flung back by rock. It sounds unhurried, and violent.

The others must be halfway down the valley by now. I am pretending that I have dropped off the radar, but I know my parents are going along with this and I feel safe up here on my own. I am nine years old, an in-between age, and I appreciate my parents' tact. The red cattle have trampled a labyrinth of paths amongst the vegetation; I follow one of them to a dead end. There was another downpour a little while ago, drenching and salty on my face, and the sun is coming out again and the world smells moist and earthy. The twisting woody heather, the hollow ground: it thuds here even when damp. One or two gorse bushes are in bloom, and though the day is cool I am sure that I can smell the golden coconut scent. The cattle are some way off just now, hanging around the dark entrance to the concrete bunker. Lumps of whitish quartz like back teeth stick out here and there, and heaps of soft grass at the top of the valley are spiky with last year's leftover stalks.

I always expect the valley to reveal itself gradually, and always it catches me unawares. There, below, are the stream and the cove. What I see is familiar and a little unreal, like something from a film that stayed with me, or perhaps a dream. The rocky shapes come and go in the waves.

The opposite side is scored with paths, most of them straight. From a roughly semicircular gouge some way up the slope, one path leads inland along the valley and several radiate to the edge of the cliff. I've decided that these are Roman paths because we have done the Romans at school and I know they built straight roads. It follows that this semicircle was once a turning place for chariots; that the paths are narrow and the slope dizzying is neither here nor there. Above the turning place the valley ends in those sheer oblong rockfaces. Further down it forms a low cliff around the cove, with paths to explore and places like my ledge where, at high tide, I can sit right above the waves. Still further down is a rectangular foundation. It's the same shape as the foundation at Lullingstone and therefore must have been a Roman villa. One side is a matter of feet from the cliff edge, a strange place for a villa when you think about it. Wherever I look there is slate, heaps and strewn patches and remnants of wall. Low banks begin and end nowhere in particular, and the stream has small cliffs all of its own. There is not another valley like this in the whole world.

The path before me is steep and narrow. It glitters with a hundred thousand fragments of slate and has different ways of being treacherous. In dry weather, when the ground is dusty, the tiny slates slip under your feet. If you put your weight in the wrong place you slide on your heels, and it is the helpless falling, falling that happens when you are just about asleep: you crash awake, and your heart is pounding and you have no idea why. When it rains, as it has done today, or a special fog rolls in from the sea and soaks the world stealthily, the slates become if not exactly wet, then greasy and unpredictable. Damp heather crowds in from either side, and I cannot resist putting my hand lightly to a bit of gorse, feeling the tips of the rigid prickles, daring one to puncture my skin. When the path passes close to the edge I am conscious, though I cannot see over it, that the cliff tilts very steeply into the sea. Whether by instinct or indoctrination I take a few steps inland and scramble down the grassy side until the path angles back again and broadens to an old track above the wreckers' cottage.

My mother, as always, is the first down. She is already striding across the bridge, Treacle at her heels. She has tied her Guernsey sweater around her waist, and her head is thrown back and she is swinging her arms. She looks . . . free, in a way that I cannot articulate. My mother loves this place.

I am looking down into the cottage now. The roof is long gone, the floor of grass. The cottage faces out across the cove, built into a nook between the valley side and a rocky outcrop at the seaward edge. It's just as well that a path runs along the back, for in front there is a mere strip of grass and thrift and then a long drop into the cove: if this wall were still standing, in fact, you might step out of your front door and straight over the cliff. These days only the rear wall and bits of the ends remain. Sometimes, when rain really sets in and the tide is too high for us to reach the shelter of the cave, we huddle in a corner here to eat our lunch. I squeezed into a chimney breast on one occasion but it smelled of cigarette butts and old satsuma peel. The worst of the weather blows over our heads, straight inland, and although this too is an unusual place in which to build a home, I understand completely why you might choose to live here, not just near but right at the ocean and its thrilling weather. I know that if I could lie in bed, the front door locked tight, the sea just the other side of the wall, and breathe this air and listen to this wildness, I would sleep soundly every night.

But about that deadly drop from the vanished front door – it is reason enough for the cove to be haunted, or would be if we did ghosts in our family – why would you build your home right on the edge of the cliff unless you were a wrecker? My mother read Daphne du Maurier one holiday, and told me about the wreckers in *Jamaica Inn*: how they flashed lanterns to lure ships onto the rocks of this northern coast, and waited for the tide to bring in goods from the wreckage, and killed any survivors who washed ashore with the booty. It is obvious to me that wreckers lived here. The rocks below are treacherous, and you could ply your deadly trade – flash a lantern, wreck a ship – from your very own doorstep. The mast-light drawing closer to the light on the cliff, I read for myself, 'fascinated and held, like a moth coming to a candle'. You would easily get your plunder back up the track with a small cart and a donkey or sure-footed pony.

I am not to go to the wreckers' cottage alone, but I leave the path a little further on and step straight down the slope. Sideways, as I have watched my father do, a stretching downward step with the outer foot and a short, halting one with the inner foot; I've worked out that you must never, ever let your feet cross. I like the sense of daring and the slight giddiness – you could fall a long way if you lost your footing here – and above all I love the way my body has to work with the steepness and the bumps. It makes me feel that I am really here.

At the bottom I will clamber along by the stream and cross the stone bridge, and make my way amongst the lumps and little earthy cliffs, the sudden windless corners, over to the villa. I'll climb down into the foundation – it is littered with tiny pieces of slate, and practically as deep in one corner as I am tall – and then I will scramble up and over into the secret path. It is narrow, and I always pick it up as it emerges from a kind of bridge or tunnel that doesn't work as either. If it is a bridge, it leads nowhere; considered as a tunnel the rectangular opening is too small for a person though I think a sheep would fit. The path then passes directly above the sheltering, fishy-smelling cave. The valley side rises like a wall to the right; to the left is the crumbly cliff edge, and it is generally better not to look down. I always hurry across that part. Maybe it is my imagination, but whenever I walk along it the path seems slightly narrower than it did before. Then it leads between walls of rock that never see the sun, and glisten and trickle noisily. There is light ahead, and the green shade plants give way to thrift. Thrift belongs to the brightness of the sea.

I will come out onto my ledge directly above the cove. You feel that you could climb down to the rocks from there, but the drop is just a bit too high and very much too sheer. And anyway, my ledge is like a little cove. You are tucked into the cliff like a nesting gull, slapped and pounded by the wind, cloistered from the land, and you can look indefinitely out to sea. Sometimes, when the tide has chased us out of the cove, I sit there and watch water surge where not so long before we ate our sandwiches and pottered about, and my parents looked at the sea or read, and I found a perfect pebble and watched a dog whelk inch its way around a shallow pool. I won't stay long on the ledge today, for the tide is going out, the wet rocks multiplying before my eyes, and soon my mother will be calling us and we will start to make our way down through the gulley.

A strange lump of slate lies on my ledge. It is fashioned into the shape of a giant book, an old-smelling, leather-bound one; the edges are even scored with grooves and ridges like pages. The book is closed, but it must have been set down recently because the pages have not quite settled shut; I like that attention to detail. I do not know who made this book of slate, nor why they left it there.

Having decided that the ruined cottage was something to do with wreckers, I did not care to speculate further. The legal subtleties of flotsam and jetsam passed me by, as did the logic of flashing lights. I added *Tales of the Cornish Wreckers* to my collection of Tor Mark booklets, but unlike the volumes on shells and flowers, this one is still in mint condition; I certainly never got through an entire tale. What captured my imagination was the cottage on the edge of the cliff, as close to the cove, the ocean, as a cottage could be without not being at all. A cottage in which you might sleep soundly – as, and this did not occur to me at the time, you ought not to if you had the blood of shipwreck victims on your hands. It was the same with the Roman paths and the villa, broad-brush stuff: my theories did not once touch upon an imagined population in togas and chariots. As for the sheep tunnel, it never occurred to me to wonder why, with a whole valley for the grazing, you might build a tunnel that would effectively conduct your livestock over the edge of a cliff. Beyond the fact that people had inhabited and shaped the valley in all kinds of ways, I was incurious. Their traces belonged to the landscape, like the tumuli and the bunker up on the common, and the solitary brick tower. The identities that I conferred on them were a kind of private cartography: they enabled me to think and talk my way around the place.

Why don't you write a legend about The Mountain? my mother suggested once. I was, after all, seldom without a notebook of some kind. We were climbing up from Tregardock, going to the cove, and had paused to look back at the bracken-covered crag; it was, we both agreed, the sort of place that a giant might frequent. Maybe, I said, watching the wind make silver of the ferniness, and the story ended there. I got on with roaming and rummaging, wading and peering, sitting looking. I filled my notebooks with observations, and the names of plants and shells. I could not care less about smugglers and Romans and giants, least of all a mythical king up at Tintagel, where we went one afternoon to fill up with petrol. What I really cared about was the sea and, at the edge of the sea's immensity, the cove. I want to write about this, I told my mother as we sat on a low-tide rock, the water lapping, but I don't know how. I don't know how to put it all into words.

I do not recall thinking very much at all as I looked out to sea: the line of the horizon, how many miles of ocean extended to it, what lay beyond it, though I must have wondered in passing whether my mother had packed the lemon cake. It did not occur to me that beyond the vastness lay the further vastness of Canada. I certainly could not have dreamed that, there and then, the axis of my life extended 3,800 miles due west – within three quarters of a latitudinal degree – through the Great Northern Peninsula of Newfoundland to a terrestrial ocean, the prairie, where a small boy with a gigantic laugh, my future husband, played street hockey.

The sea absorbed me: it mattered for itself. The cove was the cove. I knew what I needed to know about it, and that remained the case for roughly the next forty years.

*

I have not been down into Beacon Cove, another place that I used to love, since the cliff collapsed when I was ten years old. Beacon Cove is edged with rocks, spacious with sand, wrapped around by lofty cliffs, and because the Atlantic breakers are long and their barrelling approach unchecked, the cove contains a special vigorous echo – at least, that is how I remember it. To get there you walked along the cliffs from Mawgan Porth, and turned off on a path that zigzagged down the steepening cliff. Trollope would have approved heartily of the place; cliffs, he asserted with reference to his fictional cove, 'should be nearly precipitous, they should be broken in their outlines, and should barely admit here and there of an insecure passage from the summit' to 'the sand at their feet'.

When you were still quite some way from the bottom, the grass and thrift gave way to rock. The path paused here, turned sharp right, and continued along the edge of the rockface to a man-sized hole through which you peered onto sand and rocks below. The path formed a kind of causeway around the hole, a significant drop on the other side – seven careful steps – and then it entered a massive angular recess that, I now realise, must have been quarried from the cliff. You crossed this recess on a narrow ledge, one foot after the other, singing loudly for some reason, slate rising sheer to your right and dropping sheer from your left. *I can see clearly now the rain has gone.* At the far side the slate fell away more gradually – I needed help climbing down this part when I was small, and my mother had to pass Treacle down into my father's arms – and then it levelled out and became wave-smoothed, and faded into sand. *Here is that rainbow I've been praying for* . . . I tore off my boots and socks and ran full pelt to the edge of the sea. It was all ours for the duration of a tide; we seldom saw other people here.

   . . . gonna be a bright, bright sunshiny day.

The narrow causeway seemed to narrow further over time, though it was difficult to say for sure; the hole certainly expanded to more than one man's girth. I remember walking around the coast from Mawgan Porth on a brilliant and very windy day, my head full of Beacon Cove: the firm wet sand, the likelihood of finding a cobalt-blue glass stone, the long, long rolling waves, the special elevated sound. My mother was in front as usual, hurrying down the zigzagging path, along the edge, Treacle at her heels, and then she stopped dead because the hole had gone, the fragile causeway too, and the path ended in air.

I think my mother had a close call that morning. My parents never spoke of that moment again, and I have no recollection of where we spent the rest of the day. I do remember climbing back up the cliff and feeling what in years to come I would recognise as grief: I knew that I would never set foot in Beacon Cove again, that this magical place now belonged to the oystercatchers. I saw them flying fast and low above the waves, breaking (as I liked to think) the speed of their own sound. *Pip pip pip pip pip*: it trailed behind them, echoing.

Someone told me that there is a new way down to Beacon Cove and that it involves the use of ropes. But that sort of thing is beyond me, and besides I have no business there any more. Since that day I have been back to the top of the old path just once, when Shaun and I took our first trip to Cornwall together. When I looked down on the cove its distance in time felt like geographic distance, as if it were not a mere eighty metres below but an image brought close by a very powerful telescopic lens. Twenty years away in light like amber, vitrified and wonderful.

I am glad these memories were wrapped up in their special light before I read that a rowing boat containing ten frozen corpses drifted ashore at Beacon Cove in the winter of 1846. They were buried locally, in a grave marked with the stern of their boat, a sad, perfect monument; the novelist Wilkie Collins saw it when he hiked around Cornwall barely four years later. Collins describes the dead as local fishermen, but it seems rather that they were shipwrecked off the coast of Ireland, surviving to suffer days of further terror and deaths by starvation and hypothermia. You don't input from the supernatural for a fact like that to haunt Beacon Cove. It is there, one way or another, in the place's memory.

I do not know what to think about those edges and drops, that widening hole; they too are encapsulated in my past, untested by adult experience, though the crumbled cliff and the broken-off path are real enough. Did we enjoy those days of charmed seclusion down in Beacon Cove because other people thought the access too dangerous, or just too much effort? Why did I sing loudly every time I trotted along that ledge? Why, given the excitement and insouciance with which I followed Treacle and my mother down, do I look at a discoloured photograph that my father took with his trusty Halina and think that, were the path still intact, I quite possibly would not take it today? Were those worries that I left behind in Sussex the work of brain chemistry alone, or did they know something I did not about the places I loved? They had, after all, predicted that the path would give way, and so it had come to pass.

These things do not appear to have been on my mind the day after my mother nearly stepped off the cliff. We walked to the cove today, I wrote on a postcard to my maternal grandparents, and ate our lunch in the wreckers' cottage because it was raining. There were nine cormorants on the cormorants' rock. Yesterday we went to Beacon Cove, but the path had collapsed. Mummy was in front. Love, Beth XXXXX PS Hope the guinea pigs are well! PPSS There are piglets at Tregardock! On the front of the postcard, in 1970s colour made lurider by time, are donkeys on the beach at Bude. We had never been to Bude, but I liked the photo of the donkeys.

*

When I am in Cornwall, I often carry addressed and stamped postcards around with me, passing more convenient mailing opportunities, until I can get to my favourite letterbox. It is a slender Victorian affair, the slot just wide enough for a standard 4×6-inch card, set into a farm wall at the head of the valley high above my cove. The lock surround has corroded away – salt weather is hard on a letterbox – though the lock is still in use and mail is collected at 11.45 a.m. from Monday to Saturday. The letters 'VR' stand out in three dimensions, divided by a chunky crown. Oxidation and slapped-on paint have taken their toll – but once upon a time the box and its livery would have been cutting edge. It may well not have been red to begin with, but a shade of muted green that today would be described as 'heritage'. In the 1850s, thanks in no small measure to Anthony Trollope, future author of the Barsetshire novels, the British postal system was revolutionised by the introduction of letter-boxes – first the pillar box and then a wall-recessed version. To begin with the boxes were that subtle green colour, tasteful and discreet to a fault. Tradition has it that Victorians bumped into them and sustained injuries, but a more prosaic explanation is that letterboxes lose much of their point if they are hard to find – lost amongst the crowds of a London street, or camouflaged in a green Cornish lane. In 1874 work began to repaint the boxes red, the opposite of inconspicuous. The colour 'pillar-box red' was born and letterboxes everywhere, like this one, became minor landmarks: you follow the lane for about half a mile, and turn left at the letterbox.

It is not unlikely that, one day in 1851, someone at the farmhouse behind this wall answered the door to a booming, bespectacled man attired in jodhpurs and a red hunting jacket, possibly still mounted on his horse, who introduced himself as Anthony Trollope. The aspiring novelist had a day job as surveyor's clerk for the Post Office, and in the early 1850s was detailed to oversee the expansion and regularisation of the postal network in rural Britain – to 'cover the country', as he put it, 'with rural letter-carriers' and thereby 'catch all recipients of letters'. In this capacity, Trollope spent two years riding around the west and south-west of the island, interrogating rural post-masters about the journeys of the letters that passed through their hands and doorstepping householders in out-of-the-way places to enquire (a forward question in days before the letter-box brought anonymity) how, and at what cost, they sent and received their mail. He rode in the company of his groom, av-eraging forty miles a day, indulging his passion for fox hunting at every opportunity, and later claimed to have visited 'every nook', 'almost every house' in the region. It is hard to imagine a richer education for a novelist. Within three years of his return not only was a comprehensive postal system in the making, but Trollope had published his first major novel. *The Warden* originated in the Salisbury leg of his West Country tour, and as the letterbox network expanded so too did his fictional project, novel by novel, into the six-book *Chronicles of Barsetshire* on which Trollope's literary reputation rests.

The farm behind the wall at Trebarwith changed hands in the year of Trollope's probable visit; the occupants may thus have had years of postal tribulations to share with him or, being newcomers, virtually none. Because 1851 also happened to be a census year, a fairly reliable record exists of the hamlet's population at the time. The majority of inhabitants recording an occupation worked in the local slate industry: thirteen slate quarrymen and five slate 'makers' or sawers, or cutters. There were also two stone masons; five agricultural labourers; two sand carriers, one of whom was blind; a handful of servants; the farmer, of course; and two paupers. The return also, intriguingly, lists two uninhabited cottages down in the valley.

Before the surveyor's clerk got as far as Salisbury he saw melodramatic potential in those 'bold' and 'precipitous' cliffs between Tintagel and Bossiney. Malachi, the elderly protagonist of Trollope's Cornish story, does not live at his eponymous cove, he lives in it. The home that he shares with his granddaughter is a makeshift structure built on rock close to the high-tide mark, and the pair eke out a precarious existence – as some did here-abouts in the nineteenth century – by collecting seaweed and selling it for agricultural fertiliser. Trollope's tale of people at the outermost edges of the land and of society is hardly a work of social conscience: it is highly romanticised, written from a place of economic and physical security. As for the surveyor's clerk's official job, the village of Tintagel – then still named Trevena – was yet to be opened up by tourism, and this rural region of slate and weather, of quarries and hamlets and far-flung farmsteads, seaweed and sand, would have been grist to his mill. He would have found his way through the lanes and over fields to the south of Tintagel, and in the detailed notes that consumed his daily writing time might very plausibly be imagined specifying the location of the letterbox at Trebarwith.

The last time I posted something here a heart-shaped piece of moss had appeared in the wall. It was bulging and asymmetric like a real heart, and so vibrantly green against the pillar-box red, its complementary colour, that you might be forgiven for thinking, momentarily, that you could see it beat.

*

There are edges and there are edges, ways of falling and ways of falling.

A few days after my eleventh birthday, the Japanese anemones in bloom, I encountered danger. I started secondary school, a mediocre single-sex establishment, and I was bullied from day one. The slope on which I found myself was slippery, but this time there was no one to hold me safe by a figurative bit of clothing.

I suspect it is not unusual for victims of bullying to find ways of accounting for – justifying, of all things – why they have been singled out. Not only was I a confirmed little sister, I was about as young in my school cohort as one could be and, by any standards, fairly naive. I'd always been a soft target for practical jokes because if someone told me something I was apt to believe them; I still am. What I lacked in age I made up for in size; I was conspicuously tall, a little overweight, clumsy and scared of balls in a culture that took the ability to catch or hit one as the norm. Being on the bookish side didn't help. Even so, I will never understand what happened in that first week. I set off in my new, grown-up uniform, mildly apprehensive but brimful of excitement at what lay ahead: proper subjects like French and chemistry, the dream of turning out to be OK at hockey, of making friends and above all just fitting in. By the Friday I was scared out of my life, and when Monday morning came around and my father was starting up the car I ran back into the house and was violently ill. Thus began a good many school days for the next two years. I woke before five most mornings and crept out to spend time with the pony, often riding in the lighter months; just once my mother heard me transporting my saddle and clobber in the wheelbarrow, and sent me back to bed. I cherished the car journeys with my father, our regular programmes on Radio 4, my father's kindness and our long conversations about the pony and photography, music and the origins of words – but when he dropped me off at the sickly-blue gate and headed on to work I knew myself to be in danger.

This is how I came to like corners.

Apart from the evening when we went to A & E because somebody had sprained my thumb, I spared my parents most of what was said and done – or maybe it was that I spared myself the humiliation of telling them, for such is the bully's genius that there was one kind of shame in being the centre of terrible attention, and another in the personalised specifics of how that attention was paid. I did not tell anyone, not even the pony to whom I told many things, and I never will.

Every evening, when we got home, I washed my hands thoroughly but never quite cleansed them of whatever had happened to me that day. My mother reluctantly allowed me to keep my uniform and bag by the back door, away from my bedroom; she was bemused, but knew strength of feeling when she encountered it. I wish that I could thank the three fifth formers with whom I walked to the canteen, a dangerous route, and the sixth-form art student who encouraged me to spend the remainder of each lunch hour in the pottery room. At first I perched on a stool and watched as she manipulated and scraped and smoothed exquisite organic forms from clay. The tiny room was a haven, the cold smell of clay, the way sun streamed through the dirty window, the generous unspoken understanding. I began to experiment with clay myself, and eventually made a pot that we both agreed was good enough to fire and glaze. Before my creation had air dried, however, someone gained access to destroy the thing, making it known that there was nowhere on the premises to hide.

Then, one Sunday afternoon, I heard voices in the front garden and a familiar numbness set into my face, a ringing in my ears, and my vision blurred momentarily. My mother came back into the kitchen. Two girls were at the gate. They said they were friends of mine, they'd come to see me. No! I said, no! But they say they've cycled miles, you'll have to invite them in. No! I don't understand, my mother said. Please, just no! My mother got it. We went to the gate together and I thought I was about to die, but the girls put on a show of charm and eventually they left. That evening, at lights-out, I checked under the bed. Home was not as safe as it ought to have been.

The cove was the safest place in the world. The wrapping cliff, the measureless ocean. Cloud shadows scudding across the valley floor. A whitish pebble in the palm of my hand: it was cold and hard and intensely heavy, and it glistered when I held it up to the light. The way whelks did not quite slide nor yet quite drift around a rock pool, but appeared to glide fractionally above the bottom as you might expect a ghost shell to do. The light and the sound of the place, the salt. The rocks, their marvellous shapes and the recesses amongst them. How the waves heaved and broke on them and made me absolutely calm inside. How the cove was the wildest place imaginable and how it was my place, more than home itself. How I felt free and happy here and, treading its narrow edges, safe. My slaty ledge and the solitude. Solitude is not loneliness: it is freedom to think and notice, to be yourself. If you are solitary, then by definition nobody can get at you.

*

And the cove had to be kept safe, at all costs. That defining sense of holiday as time out from the everyday had become the difference between feeling safe and being in danger. Cornwall could not under any circumstances be alluded to at school – and to mention school in Cornwall would be an act of irreparable contamination, the cove catastrophically compromised. The cove had to be kept innocent. It is true that my interior discourse was rather less amenable to censorship.

My mother and I took long walks around the edges of our Cornish days, living up every first and last modicum of daylight. Sometimes it seemed to me that each moment might, by being fully inhabited, somehow be stretched and time thereby slowed, the painful journey out of Cornwall further deferred. We walked the cliff path to Trevose Head after dinner, into the sunset, returning at dusk through inland lanes in time for *M*A*S*H*, or we set off for Padstow at dawn, a two-hour walk around the coast towards the rising sun. I remember the early sandy bay, the world all ours, the sheer joy of watching a dog run for the sheer joy of it. The softness of the light as we walked into Padstow, the harbour getting going, my father waiting with the car. Back to the flat, the others getting up, and then the smell of bacon frying.

These walks were precious times, precious spaces, touched with special candour on my mother's part as if she were liberated from roles and rules, and didn't care or had forgotten that I was only eleven or twelve and had my own, junior, role in the family. Subjects that were off-limits back at home were freely discussed as we pounded the coast path: my grandmother's unfortunate marriage, my mother's wartime childhood. How I very nearly hadn't happened at all because, when he was thirty-three, they thought my father was going to die. My mother's exasperation with a difficult relative whom we all appeased in everyday life, and her receptiveness to my own strong feelings on the matter. How my mother, a talented potter, dreamed of leaving her teaching career to set up a studio. How, which was news to me, she and my father had very nearly moved us all to Cornwall a year or two before; how I wished we had made the move, and how I was glad that we hadn't, because I would have missed my grandmother. How, one day, my mother and I would own the red-brick tower in the field above the cove. There would be windows in the sightless apertures, and at each window a chair or two, and cattle grazing right up to the door. We'd need a camping stove to boil water, and notebooks, pens, digestive biscuits. Torches, I said, and Turkish Delight. Hot-water bottles, my mother said. Only one subject remained off-limits: we might have put the world substantially to rights, but by unspoken mutual consent school was never, ever mentioned.

On a beach you might step down to the water's edge. Here in the cove there is no such thing, just rock pools enlarging to sea. I waded out amongst the rocks and the cold, cold water thrilled along my nerves like life itself. The tangle of oarweed around my legs, its heave and drain with each laborious step, the exhilarating undertow that pushed you around, knocked you off balance, made you completely and utterly alive. The unseen things beneath my feet: leathery seaweed, hard limpet tips. Mussels with edges like blunt blades. Once I cut my foot on something and blood ribboned like red crinkleweed in the shifting water.

*

The cove is not an obvious place for campfires: it is too rocky, too watery. But occasionally an autumn tide left behind muddles of seaweed and driftwood that were irresistible. We collected the driest pieces of wood, and I saved the most interesting bits to take home for my bedroom windowsill or for arty projects that never quite came to fruition. My father would light a fire on the shingle near the mouth of the cave for no reason other than that he loved lighting fires and I loved putting seaweed on fires. Strappy oarweed that looked like leather until you gathered up a slippery armful, and then it seemed to be at once faintly synthetic and almost animate. I draped huge fronds over the smoking heap, and their colour changed from ochre to an otherworldly green. Khaki wracks turned green too, the colour of plants that grow on land. Egg wrack, bladder wrack: the air sacs would smear your hands with slime should you split one open with a thumbnail, but they popped pleasingly on the occasions that a flame broke through. Our fires, coaxed from the sea's damp leavings, were salty-smouldering affairs.

Seaweeds or marine algae, like terrestrial plants, feed by photosynthesis: they harvest light through coloured pigments and convert or synthesise this energy into nutrients. The instrumental pigment is a type of chlorophyll which, because it reflects green light, gives leaves their green colour. Algae growing in all but the shallowest waters optimise available light with 'accessory' pigments that lend them their brown and red complexions. These pigments are less resistant than chlorophyll to heat and this is why, when you toss a length of oarweed onto a campfire, the orange-brown fucoxanthin degrades and you are left with the colour green.

Kelp, of which oarweed is a variety, is a common sight around

British shores. I've picked my way over Scottish beaches ankle-deep in the stuff, and waded through forests of forest kelp in Northern Ireland. The foreground of a Skye seascape that hangs in our home is plastered with thick layers of kelp colour. Of the myriad algae that thrive in the cove, it is oarweed that I see in my mind's eye when I think of this rocky intertidal place: masses of fat rubbery stems and bright-brown finger-like fronds heaped around the foot of the cliff or backed up in the cave; groves swaying in low-tide waves almost but not quite as trees sway in wind. It is oarweed that I feel too, in recollection, slapping and writhing, entangling with each exaggerated barefoot step as I wade out towards the cormorants' rock: not for nothing is oarweed also called 'sea tangle', or simply 'tangle'.

Seaweeds are the living origins of terrestrial plant life. As we know, they photosynthesise, a defining characteristic of plants: they are chlorophyll green in essence, if not always, at least until you cook them, in appearance. They attach themselves to rocks by means of holdfasts, branching growths that bring to mind the feet of fantastical clawless birds. If a loose stem of oarweed, considered from the blade end, looks not unlike an elaborate oar, it makes, with the bulbous holdfast at the other end, a serviceable if rather bendy club. The root-like tips of a holdfast can grip their way into minute cracks, and cement themselves to surfaces by means of powerful adhesive substances. Green and red algae belong to the plant kingdom; it's from the greens that, hundreds of millions of years ago, terrestrial plant life began to evolve. In most botanical opinions, however, the brown kelps and wracks are not plants at all; they are assigned to a kingdom called Chromista (from the Greek word for 'colour'), which evolved independently of the reds and greens, and more recently.

Who knows how the vast kelps and ubiquitous wracks came to be here: whether they colonised vacant habitats, or whether they arrived and multiplied like aliens or knotweed, crowding the red and green plants out into their disparate realms. Knotted wrack, bladder wrack, sugar kelp, tangle. These ancient arrivistes of the vegetative world that sequester carbon like nothing else, these photosynthesising non-plants with curious feet and in-between ways: who knows where they came from?

What if tangle originated not in salt water, but on land? 'Deep in the Forest of Tangle', wrote the twentieth-century Cornish poet Charles Causley,

> *The King of the Makers sat*
> *With a faggot of stripes for the tiger*
> *And a flitter of wings for the bat.*

'He'd a grindstone for sharpening swordfish'; 'hundreds of kangaroo-pouches'; 'hoots for the owls, and for glow-worms . . . goodness knows how many shines'. Who is the King of the Makers, and what is the reason for his prodigious output of 'hums for . . . humming-birds, buzzes for bees'; 'porcupine quills', 'a bevy of bills / And various furs for the bear'? Is he making parts and attributes for creatures that he has yet to create, or that he has created but not yet finished? Does he perhaps supply bits and pieces to another creator? Maybe the creatures, whoever their creator, are complete: maybe they've already received their finishing touches, the eels their electrical charges and the owls their hoots, and the efforts of the King of the Makers are superfluous. Or does he perhaps make for the sake of making, which in itself would account for his name? He has even made 'pectoral fins for sea-fishes / With which they might glide through the air,' as so-called 'flying fish' certainly do. But what if sea fish in general have been designed to inhabit air? Which may just be the case, for the forest of tangle shows every sign of being, in the beginning, a terrestrial one.

This is how, in Causley's poignant myth, the sea came to be, how tangle became sea-tangle: in the salt tears of loneliness, of being out of time. For

> . . . *the old King of the Makers*
> *With tears could have filled up a bay,*
> *For no one had come to his warehouse*
> *These many long years and a day.*
>
> *And sadly the King of the Makers*
> *His bits and his pieces he eyed*
> *As he sat on a rock in the midst of his stock*
> *And he cried and he cried and he cried.*
> *He cried and he cried and he cried and he cried,*
> *He cried and he cried and he cried.*

Maybe the King of the Makers has a cloak of tangle, like the one I am wearing in a photograph taken long before I'd heard of Charles Causley. I am standing barefoot on a rock, the lower flanks of which are scrubby with wrack and calcareous with barnacles. Rocks sprawl and rise behind me, mussels gleaming darkly. The cormorants' rock and the composite snail are fully revealed; the sea beyond is blue, idyllic low tide. My jeans are rolled up for paddling and, draped dripping around my shoulders like some Prospero's cast-off, hangs glossy, leathery, raggedy oarweed. I'm eleven years old and have a new hairstyle with which I was pleased until I went back to school; my unruly hair had been a source of mockery but so, it turned out, was the new short crop. I cannot read my expression after all these years: it belongs to me and it does not. Life is not easy, I know that much, but here, at this moment in the cove, I must surely be on top of the world.

Back then, even were I so inclined, there was no question of helping myself to growing seaweeds, for they stuck to rocks like the limpets that set up home amongst their holdfasts and their fronds. The cove was fairly clear about what could and could not be harvested. The empty shells and loose weed and wood that washed up, the fishing buoys and bits of net were there for the taking between the tides, and then everything would be washed away again together with some half-cooked kelp and the ashes of our campfire. We came and then we went, but the cove was the cove. It would be there for us next time not because it cared, but because it was there.

That said, whenever I returned I had a vague feeling that I was expected. Perhaps this was inevitable, such was my own spilling anticipation, a sense of connection so strong that it might be assumed – unthinkingly, feelingly – to be reciprocal. It was as if the cove were somehow waiting, listening.

*

At thirteen I moved to a school in another town. It was not quite the fresh start it ought to have been, for a former classmate made the same move and set about gaining influence; I suppose I should be grateful that I did not go to school in an age of social media. I kept going, by working hard. O level English turned me inside out, for the first of our set texts was *Macbeth*. My heart went out to the somnambulant Lady Macbeth as she went through the motions of scrubbing and lathering hands that would 'ne'er be clean': no matter that she had metaphorical blood on them, I knew what it was like to be haunted, tormented by a thing that could not be washed away. Then, which was rather below the belt, we did *Lord of the Flies*. At last, in the sixth form, there were departures and arrivals, and gradually fear muted to vigilance: I found friends. I had loving parents; a kind, wise grandmother; my old friend Mrs G, with whom I maintained a lively correspondence. For a while I had Sophie, the cantankerous loaned pony who kicked and bit when I saddled up but saved me from losing my young mind. And I had Cornwall, the cove where I was safe. Somehow I got my grades and a place to read English at university. I survived.

I did not see Cornwall for a while after I went off to university. In retrospect I missed the cove terribly, but I barely noticed at the time: I was too busy working too hard and worrying that I was a fraud unworthy of a place at Cambridge. Whilst waiting to be found out on that count I haunted libraries at silly hours, laboured through reading lists unselectively, thought until I'd no idea how to think, and burned out. I took a leave of absence and spent a bohemian interlude selling second-hand books; I got better again. When I returned to take my final year I would work hard but not too hard, and get my degree while having a huge amount of fun.

*

Not long before the start of that last academic year, my mother rang to say that she and my father, both now retired, had managed to book Flat 1 at rather short notice and wouldn't it be lovely if I could join them? I'd be back in Cambridge by the end of September, in plenty of time for term, and they could always put me on a train at Bodmin if I really couldn't spare the whole week. I found someone to stand in for me at the bookshop, packed some reading for a paper on Milton, and headed down to Sussex.

We set off west at the end of the day, my parents and I and an exuberant Boxer called Alice. I wound down my back-seat window as we crossed the Tamar after midnight. Wind caught and smacked at the aperture, too big to squeeze inside. I knew that it blew from the far-off sea, and I knew that tomorrow we would go to the cove. We pulled up in the small hours, the old conspiratorial crunch on gravel. A full moon, ocean on the air. I hurried up the slate steps to inspect the flat: the same old smell, a new three-piece suite, the same glazed doors, their glittery handles, my dressing table with the little drawer. We unpacked the car. Alice went out and came back in, and my parents went to bed. Alice did not. She sat by the front door, watching me. Night Alice. On your bed now. I switched off the light. Moon-shine flooded in. I turned on the light again and fetched my coat. OK, I said, let's go.

I didn't bother with a torch. We threaded our way amongst dark shapes of pampas grass and cordylines. The night lane whitish, the gate, the path, the sandy cliff and *there's the sea*! The beach seemed to stretch away forever, strangely visible, and then I saw far ahead the pale stacked lines of breaking waves, the tide as low as a tide could be. We slid and scuffled down the dunes. I took off my shoes and socks and rolled up my trousers, and we ran. The sand firm and wet beneath my feet, the stiff salt breeze. The dog skidding and hurtling: I felt her joy. The shallows glinted and were cold, and the moon picked out the foam of a spreading wave like lace in a Van Dyck portrait. We ran back and forth through the splashing water, one end of the beach to the other, the full moon and the dark-bright sea, the scrubbing salt wind, there in the moment, moment after moment. We were gone for hours.

The following day we parked at Tregardock and took the cliff path to the cove. It was a day of leaden cloud and showers and instantaneous brilliance: rainbow weather. My footsteps drummed along the path – *Tregardock Treligga Trebarwith Treknow* – and I was absolutely on top of the world. The tower in its green field, my mother striding ahead. We caught up with her at the tumuli, and because the light was perfect I took a photograph. My parents cheerful on the headland, the dog making eye contact with the lens, the sea and the sky and the west behind them. I did not know at the time just how precious an image I had captured.

We had a ball that week. My mother and I took our walks at dawn and into dusk, two adults now, putting the world to rights. On our last day we went back to the cove. Perhaps because the day was overcast the tower looked more abandoned than ever, the dark apertures emptier, and as we walked on across the common my mother and I resumed our old conversation: the tower needed glazing, and chairs at the windows. We would watch the ocean from the west-facing window, and from the north-facing one we would keep an eye on the cove. We'd heat soup and boil eggs on a camping stove. We would drink gin and tonic. With my mother's beloved binoculars we would zoom in on porpoises as they arced across the open sea. And this place must be dark at night. From here you'd see stars beyond stars beyond stars. Meteor showers, planetary conjunctions. Perhaps even the lighthouse at Trevose Head, out there in the fuzziness, the vanishing coastline.

Here in the light and all the weather, the green space and the ocean's infinitude, I would find a way at last of putting it into words: I'd write. Maybe, at last, I would see a rainbow here. And when Atlantic storms blew in, there in the tower, in amalgamated lashings of salt wind and salt rain, salt spray, would be a peace profounder than silence.

Hot-water bottles, my mother said.

My father was waiting for us at the tumuli. It was too dull for photographs. My mother was the first to walk on amongst the gorse and heather. At the time it was such an unremarkable thing to do. I'm watching her now, in my mind's eye, as I have done many times since that day. Any minute now she'll reach the top of the valley and then, for the very last time in her life, she will find herself looking down on the cove. And then, just like that, she will disappear over the brow.

II

Tumulus

Shaun and I drove west on a September day that was ridiculously, marvellously hot. We'd been together for a year, quietly engaged for much of that time, and following months of hard budgeting had recently formalised the matter with a ring; Shaun had insisted on a ring. But he had still not seen Cornwall, let alone made the cove's acquaintance. A trip was overdue.

I cannot say what I felt when we crossed into Cornwall, KERNOW, and warm air pushed in through the open windows. The clichés pertaining to a heart – that you think it might break, or that it is full – endure because they are spot on. Rough Tor – *there it is!* – and then the road along the edge of the moor, the way to the Atlantic. A first glimpse from the coast road – *there's the sea!* – and there, out of nowhere, was Rumps Point. As we drove, silent now, amongst the hedgebanks and umbelliferous verges, I kept an eye open for the clifftop church. What, I wondered suddenly, must it be like to see this longed-for landscape for the very first time? I'd ask Shaun that question another day.

We checked into a guest house in an unfashionable quarter

of Padstow, and then I drove us south from one haunt to another. Trevone, where the highest tides might lurch and slosh across the path and rough seas did not crash on rocks but were detonated thereby. Harlyn, the beach that I combed endlessly, on which I ran and wandered at first light, the world asleep, two biscuits in my pocket, or under a full moon as in a dream. The straight bright road to Trevose Head, the lighthouse, sea to either side; how I used to walk it with my mother at dusk. How, one evening, the revolving light was the exact rose-amber of the western sky as if the sunset originated in and were projected by Fresnel lenses. The waves at Porthcothan, their perennial misting. And Mawgan Porth: Betty's, the beach shop where, when I was small, I blew my pocket money on a pink inflatable dolphin; I disowned the thing almost as soon as I'd bought it, for it had an unnatural grin and an overpowering plastic smell, and contained two jingle bells that I decided were beneath me, babyish. The airy cliff path to the top of Beacon Cove, the lovely sand untrodden and untreadable below. You climbed down *there*? said Shaun.

We walked back high above the sea, everything shimmering, the sun shifting downwards, its heat intensifying. Shaun proposed a dip when we got back to the beach. We couldn't, I said, we hadn't packed our swimming things, and in any case we just – well – couldn't. That we might actually swim in the Atlantic had not occurred to me, for my parents holidayed out of season. I had always been by the ocean, at it, above it: I'd only been in it once or twice, briefly and by accident. But as we descended back into Mawgan Porth dayglo letters in the window of Betty's announced an end-of-season sale. Together, without a word of discussion, we headed for the door. What remained in the sale was there for a reason, but we kitted ourselves out for a song and hurried to the beach. Under my jeans and top a lurid flamingo stretched across my front.

We ran into the spreading splashing shallows. I felt sand drain from under my feet as the waves dragged back. The water was freezing. Shaun plunged in and swam as though water were his proper medium. He surfaced: come on, it's lovely. It's freezing. It's lovely. It's freezing. It's lovely. I waded on into the breakers, bobbing and wincing as the water reached my thighs, my waist, until I tripped or was pushed, and fell. Shaun was right: the water was lovely. Now, for the first time in my life, I was immersed in the ocean. The vigorous waves and the saltiness: it scrubbed my skin and burned my sinuses and made me feel renewed.

I think I had expected pure nostalgia on that first afternoon. But the waves were about much more than sharing with Shaun the places of those magical family holidays. They had to do with something new and newly affirmative: being here with Shaun, discovering Cornwall and the future together. They were about us.

As we walked back up the beach I shivered with cold and happiness. Ah, said Shaun, we don't have towels.

The next day billowed and shifted with clouds. The sun lit their edges and beamed through rents. It intensified the colours of the land as we climbed up out of Tregardock. The heather pinks; gorse not quite yellow nor yet quite gold, the colour of itself.

I told Shaun about argentiferous galena, a delicious name for the lead-and-silver ore that runs beneath Tregardock. How, once upon a time, a shaft was bored thirty fathoms beneath the shore, and how the adit or entrance at the foot of the cliff was fitted with a wooden door to prevent storm swells and high spring tides from flooding the mine. How a wooden door that shut out the sea was the sort of thing a mermaid might unlock in some Atlantic fairy tale.

I also carried a special heaviness to the cove. It rose and fell and churned inside, but as our path wound up through gorse I felt the old exaltation, the absolute aliveness. It was as if my body were hardwired to be in this place. The thudding path at the top of the valley, the worn slate stile, the open cliff and enormous sea. We paused, tasting the salty air. Rumps Point, Puffin Island. As we walked on my thumb felt for the ring's underside; the gold was soft and lovely to touch. Tintagel Church came into view and Shaun, who grew up landlocked, in the middle of Canada, observed that the silhouette was like nothing more than a ship setting sail on a prairie. A small, persistent wind had set in and jerky waves were texturing the sea. Rain showered in odd bursts for thirty, fifty seconds, and stopped. There, in the middle distance, was the tower – something from the war? I'd wanted to climb it since forever – and here was the field into which, just the once, I trespassed to pick mushrooms. Past the sheltered hollow where primroses grow. The path ahead rising now, the ripe grass, wild carrot going to seed. Soon the little church would reappear, and the last stretch of coast before the cove would be laid out in front of us: the common, the heather accumulating to the headland and the tumuli. I hurried on ahead, and at the top of the rise I froze.

The rainbow reached out of a place on the other side of the headland. It arched up and over the sea, red to violet, brilliant, and broke off a little way into its descent.

It's coming from the cove!

My body had forgotten how to breathe. My lungs were working hard, harder still, and I was drowning in the salt air.

Shaun took my hand. Your mom was expecting you, he said.

Exactly a year previously, my mother was dying. She was young. She fell ill days before my graduation, which she missed. At first we were assured that she had hepatitis, but it turned out to be stage 4 pancreatic cancer. I deferred my master's degree for a year and found a pub job in Cambridge so that I could be around; I am glad I did. I spent a great many hours on the road between Cambridge and Sussex in the following months.

The last weeks of my mother's life were desperate, precious ones. I find it strange that they are not a blur, quite the contrary. That extreme time separates out into instants of absolute clarity, every detail lived in the moment and lived again, over and over, in decades to come. I am there now, with my father at the dining table, writing out medication schedules on graph paper with coloured pens lest we miss or duplicate a dose. Sitting with my mother at the garden table learning how to take cuttings from the plants she loved. Violas, penstemons. The afternoon sun, its solidity. I remember growing basil and making vast quantities of pesto that no one wanted to eat. Terrible episodes at the failing hospital that failed my mother. I remember when we ran out of Oramorph on a rainy Sunday afternoon, and I set off in the car with an emergency prescription, one town, one supermarket pharmacy to another; I was gone for hours and my mother was in pain.

Somewhere in the midst of it all, sent by providence, Shaun appeared in my life. More precisely, he appeared one evening in the Cambridge pub where I worked. He introduced himself and shook my hand, which struck me as extraordinarily polite. He was from Canada, a graduate student. I was from Sussex, almost a graduate student.

And my mother was dying.

I remember being with my mother. I remember the hydrangeas and the Japanese anemones. An incandescent sunset, the evenings drawing in. The human kindness of the Marie Curie nurses who joined our household near the end. How, on the last day, sensing something, the dear dog lay down at the foot of the bed and became intractable. I remember when my mother was gone, the silence and the roses on the windowsill.

It was obvious to me that my mother's ashes should be scattered in the cove: it was where, if she could not be with us in the world, she belonged. We were all traumatised. We would get through the funeral. Later, I assumed, we would carry my mother's ashes along the coast path to the cove, the people whom she loved and who loved her, and there we would take our leave of her.

I had last come this way the year before my mother died, with my parents in a week of special luminosity, of that last photograph on the headland behind which the rainbow now was rising. Since then my cove had become a place of more than grief: of something that will never be resolved nor ever be undone.

My mother's ashes were scattered at the cove. I was not there.

I felt excluded from the place, the slate, the seaweed saltiness, the listening. For a dark while it seemed unclear whether I could ever go back: whether I was permitted to, whether I could bear to.

Then again, how could I possibly be banished from my cove?
And there was Shaun: he could not share my life without at least
– what's the right word? – meeting the cove. I had to go back.

Shaun squeezed my hand. Your mom knew you were coming,
he said again.

We walked towards the rainbow. The bands of colour broad-
ened and amalgamated, and then they brightened out into
nothing. It was the loveliest thing I had ever seen, and it shook
me to the core.

For my whole life I had walked this way in rainbow weather,
on monkeys' birthdays, and the rainbow that I longed to see
– not because rainbows symbolised anything in particular, but
because they were marvellous and beautiful – had never materi-
alised. That it should have done so on this of all days, after this
of all years, from the cove of all places, was, as coincidences go,
right up there.

Here is that rainbow I've been praying for . . .

A sense of urgency drew me on. I led the way up to the
headland, hurrying now, past the tumuli, over the brow. There
was the cove. Down the valley side, slipping and skidding. Of
course I could go back. Maybe, who knows, I was even expected. Shaun had spoken in a manner of speaking – but what if,
in some slight way, the rainbow were more than coincidence?
I would take that thought out from time to time in years to
come and turn it over, hold it up to the light, and put it back
carefully.

*

The following autumn, around the anniversary of my mother's death, Shaun and I took my father to Cornwall for a few days; we did this every October thereafter for the rest of his life. He said he never felt closer to my mother than in the hours that we spent at the cove. For thirteen years, until the day that he too died, my father never stopped wanting to be with my mother; of course he didn't. Even in those years when you are young enough to believe that your family and its transactions are the very measure of normality, I knew there was something special about my parents' relationship. They really were inseparable, except by death.

The enduring grief of these annual journeys was interwoven with cheerful togetherness. My father and I set off in the car after breakfast on a Friday – Shaun would follow by train after work – and when we stopped at the Reading services for coffee and a pastry my father declared our little holiday officially under way. That lifting feeling as we made our progress west: the Wiltshire downland and the Avonmouth bridge, a flash of light on sea ahead near Weston-Super-Mare. The lovely beech-crowned hill that could, we both agreed, be modelled on a painting by Paul Nash and was the site of who knew what mysteries. A picnic lunch and another coffee on the M5 (let's have a scone, my father said, we're on holiday). The A30, the loftiness of Dartmoor to the south. Downhill, fast, to the River Tamar, KERNOW: I eased off the accelerator as we reached the bridge and opened the window, savouring those first few seconds, sniffing for the sea. We checked into one guest house or other and, after dinner, drove to Bodmin to meet Shaun from a late train. Everybody here at last, my father said as we settled in for last orders, the whole weekend ahead.

At first, though he himself was in poor health and chronic pain, my father insisted that we park at Tregardock and walk the old way to the cove, down past the pigsty, the ferns, the black-thorn, up behind The Mountain through gorse to the clifftop, past the tower and the tumuli, down the steep valley side. Determination carried him, but even so there was no question of negotiating the slippery descent through the gulley. We had, however, a uniquely sheltered spot in the lee of an earthwork by the stream. My parents used to relocate there when the tide came in: we'd settle luxuriously amongst the thrift and wiry grass, the small mounds tapestried with thyme, and eat our lemon cake. My father might smoke a cigar, and we'd soak up every last bit of sun until it dropped behind the wreckers' cottage. And, of course, there was the ledge – my ledge – which was as close as you could be to the cove without being actually in the cove.

One year it became apparent that my father would not be able to walk to the valley. We all knew what that meant – that he would never see the cove again. Then Shaun did something that had not occurred to me in the decades that I'd been coming here: he bought an Ordnance Survey map. What, he had won-dered on our first, eventful walk to the cove, was the path like in the opposite direction from Tintagel, the church? How on earth would I know? I said. I had my own triangulation points, my own ways of charting the valleys and the cliffs, and what use is a map when you know a place inside out? Granted, it rather depends on what you mean by knowing a place – but that is another matter. I'd climbed the northern side of the valley twice, three times at most in my life, and never quite looked over the brow, which was grassed and sloped off to infinity. I had no idea what lay beyond, other than the little church which might just as well have been a mirage, an optical illusion. The cove was the cove, an end in itself, and the way to it was along the uninhabited cliff from the south.

The cove slipped off the bottom edge of Shaun's 1:25000 and turned up in an inset out at sea. The northern side of the valley grew into a bulky headland beyond which, as we now saw, lay a beach and a hamlet, a vehicular road and, tantalisingly close to the sea, a graphic of an old-style beer jug betokening a pub.

In spring, in Cornwall on our own, Shaun and I drove to Tintagel and found a space in King Arthur's Car Park. We wandered along Fore Street past the pasty shop, the Old Post Office, a cheerful abundance of New Age wares, and bought ice creams and a newspaper, and a multi-headed windmill of the kind that I loved as a child and still find irresistible. Then we stepped into a quiet green lane that dipped deep and wound up again towards the sea light and the clifftop church. The rocky hedgebanks, ferns and red campion, tansy foliage promising pungency. The church gate and the slate coffin stone, slate head-stones braced against the westerly wind, a notice: 'ADDERS!!!! Keep your dog on a lead'. The slate chest tombs made my stom-ach lurch, for I feared that I might see in through the cracks. The church was real after all, slate-stone solid and self-contained as if it had grown from the slate bedrock, which to all intents and purposes it had.

The clifftop was purple with bluebells, the juxtaposed ocean bluer than ever. We walked south along the old quarry coast. The cut cliffs and agitating sea. Tracks and crisscrossing little ways, concrete slabs and bits of wall. An iron post crumbled by saline air; it was brown to the eye but stained my fingertips a fiery orange-gold. A shale heap spilled from the top of the cliff, and as we passed I felt an involuntary lurch. The body does not forget things. Mine remembers a close call on Scottish scree when my heels slid helplessly, and here it imagines, feelingly, slipping and dropping down to the sea and, within the churning water, rock.

When Tennyson first walked this way in 1848 that iron post was perhaps part of something, the cliffs a string of working quarries. Unlike his contemporaries Collins and Trollope, the poet was already a literary celebrity when he passed through Tintagel. He was seeking inspiration for a new poem about King Arthur, who according to one version of the myth was conceived in a castle on Tintagel Island. The poem would get written, to great acclaim, but Tennyson's journal entries for that trip provide scant evidence that he found inspiration on the sliced-off headland:

Sunday. Rainy and bad, went and sat in Tintagel ruins, cliff all black and red and yellow, weird looking thing. [June] 5th. Clomb over Isle, disappointed . . .

On 6 June he walked south past the coastal quarries and saw the towering scullock, and watched a ship being loaded with slate. On the seventh he moved on to Camelford in search of King Arthur's stone.

The weather was no more auspicious when Tennyson returned in August 1860, now Poet Laureate and busy with a twelve-poem Arthurian cycle titled *Idylls of the King*. 'Arrived at Tintagel, grand coast, furious rain': this visit, like his first one and many a British summer holiday, appears to have been a washout. 'Tintagel', he wrote two days later, 'Black cliffs and caves and storm and wind, but I weather it out and take my ten miles a day walks in my weather-proofs'. Hopefully the temperature was equally inclement, for there is something peculiarly unpleasant, conducive in fact to grumpiness, about hiking in waterproofs when the weather is warm; everything is sweaty, bothersome. When he strode south along the quarry path, a tall figure clad in oilskins or perhaps a state-of-the-art mackintosh, his iconic cloak hanging safely indoors, and assuming he was game for an energetic climb, Tennyson would have arrived at or walked past the cove. I wonder what it looked and sounded like then and what, if anything, the Laureate made of it. After Tintagel he went back to Camelford, where he climbed down to meditate on the supposed King Arthur's stone and fell into a stream. By the time he reached Falmouth in September the weather had improved and the poet was, according to his hostess, 'very brown after all the pedestrianising along our . . . coast'. And pedestrianising – walking – works wonders for writing: just think of the Wordsworths. As for *Idylls of the King*, when the first part was published in 1859 it put far-flung Tintagel on the tourist map and the genie was out of the bottle. I wonder what Tennyson made of that, too.

The restless sea below. We rounded a headland, and the strange towering cliffs of Trebarwith Strand swung into view. Their planes and facets brought sculpture to mind, not a piece of sculpture so much as the process of sculpting, chipping away. Slates littered level surfaces and poured down slopes, frozen in motion. Neat patches of curzeyway merged into focus amongst the slate complexity, ochres and greys. That this had been here all along, tucked behind the headland, leading to the cove. We paused on an outcrop at the end of the Strand and watched the sea push in below, its rhythms and its volumes. From this end-on vantage point the waves cast shadows like solid things.

The high path, the quarry tracks and fields and walls. The curzeyway zigzag and the idea of an adder's back. Lichens, their bluish tones and their fragile forms. A clean wound in the top of the cliff, a bit of wall hanging. Brambles. Then, through a gap, we found ourselves looking down on a huge, roughly semicircular recess in the cliff. A slate pillar towered at its centre, facing out to sea. Slate debris lay around the base of the structure as if whoever created it had just downed tools and walked away. To paraphrase Betjeman, the pillar looked exactly as though man had built it. This is the scullock that caught Tennyson's eye and put yet another Laureate, Simon Armitage, in mind of a sundial (what is it with scullocks and Poet Laureates?).

A pale building at the far end of the bay proved to be the pub. There were a few cottages, a packed car park and a beach shop selling proper seaside wares like castle-shaped buckets and fishing nets mounted on bamboo canes, a design unsurpassed by modern technology. Near-vertical flights of steps scaled the hill behind the pub. A little more than halfway up I would pause and look back down on the roofs and feel fleetingly that I was going to fall. At the top, in a high green field, we would see for miles: the common and the bunker, my red-brick tower, a scattering of slightly-inland settlements, Rumps Point and Puffin Island in haze. The cove close by and out of sight. As we crossed the field a lark would rise and I would think of my father, who often said that skylarks made his heart sing. I'd follow the airy watery song with my eyes, stage upon singing stage, up and up and up again to a fluttering speck in the sky. But first there was a pint of Tribute to be drunk.

The proximity of my secluded cove to a busy little seaside hub took me aback. It lay not far around the headland – a strenuous way on foot, admittedly, but yards away as the crow flies or the seal swims. The place that the cove occupied in the world was not what I had assumed it to be.

And, as Shaun had gathered from the map, you could drive right down to the pub above the sea at the foot of the headland. You could not get closer to the cove by land without being at the cove itself. It was a masterstroke, a gift of gifts to my father. On a mild, overcast morning in October we found our way to Trebarwith Strand on a road that descended through a narrow valley; locals call it the sanding or 'sanden' road because sand and seaweed were transported up it to fertilise and alkalinise farmers' fields. Past the quarries around Penpethy, slate spoil spilling down the steep wooded sides. Buildings and sea light ahead, the end of the road, the edge of the sea. A familiar off-shore rock loomed into view. Look, Dad. Look what Shaun's found for you. I thought I'd never see these waves again, my father said.

He could smell the waves as well, feel their salt misting as we nursed pints at a picnic table on a low outcrop above the beach. At high tide the sea churned and crashed at our feet. We sat there in most of the weather bar heavy rain that Cornish autumns put your way – once in T-shirts, memorably, more often in fleeces and jackets and hats – and watched the sea, and watched people watching the sea or chasing the tides, a dog or child running on the first revealed sand. Beyond the pub a track sloped around to a sunless sandy corner, the end of the Strand. Back in the day, slates were carted down here for loading into ships. On the brightest day it was a cold dark spot, and the waves broke with a hollow tone that made me almost shiver – but my father always took a turn down the track to be that bit closer to the cove.

In the years since my father's death the overworked cliff has subsided and the track is now closed off – and that is OK, for my father no longer has need of it. It is OK, too, for another reason: a local farmer told me that horseshoe bats roost in a cave in that dark corner when we are up and about in the day. They slumber upside down in the 'heavens', as he put it, the ceiling of their echoing cave, deep beneath our feet as we climb the headland, up and away from the hurly-burly of the beach. Their claws are locked fast by the pull of their body weight on a special tendonal mechanism; once secured, they are held in place by the total relaxation of their bodies. If the bats are not to fall, in other words, they must sleep soundly. You could say the same of a person. I wonder if they notice the sound of the sea, that hollowness; the cave must be thunderous at high tide. Maybe they find peace in the cracking and crashing, their senses at one with the elements. I wonder whether, out and about, hunting at dusk in summer, they find their way over or around the headland. I wonder what it is like in the cove during the bats' waking hours, what happens there at night.

*

A thirty-year-old architect's clerk from Dorset called Thomas Hardy also travelled the sanding road. In March 1870 he was dis-patched to St Juliot, a few miles upstream from Boscastle, where the church had fallen into disrepair. His employer, engaged to restore the building, assigned Hardy to survey the structure, make some preliminary drawings, and research building materials; he would lodge with the vicar. Hardy, who was writing a novel in his spare hours, would travel by rail to Launceston, changing three times; a hired trap would convey him the last fifteen-odd miles to St Juliot. When he arrived at the vicarage in his shabby greatcoat he was welcomed by the vicar's sister-in-law Emma, his host being indisposed with gout. Emma was a breath of fresh air, an impulsive woman who was drawn to edges and ledges and loved to feel the wind in her hair; to gallop along clifftops on her pony Fanny, which must have been intoxicating. On the second day of that brief first visit she drove Hardy by pony and trap to inspect roofing slates at Penpethy Quarry, on the sanding road, where slate of a distinctively 'greenish colour' was extracted.

Those two days in Cornwall changed Hardy's life: he returned home, he later wrote, with 'magic in [his] eyes'. He had plenty of time to think on the journey. Not only was romance stirring between Hardy and Emma, his future wife; by the time his fourth train pulled into Dorchester he was very much closer to giving up his professional prospects in architecture for the novelist's uncertain path. When Hardy returned to St Juliot he and Emma would picnic down by the river, or walk the cliffs at Beeny, north of Boscastle, or head further afield in the trap. On one of these outings Emma made a pen-and-ink sketch, now held by the New York Public Library, titled 'Gathering Seaweed. Trebarwith Strand'.

The precise vantage point of Emma's sketch is just beyond the pub, out of bounds today but close enough to the spot where we sat with my father. The artist clearly knows her thirds, a compositional principle that strives for visual harmony by dividing the canvas or page or viewfinder into three; Emma's page is divided horizontally. Massed rocks cut across the bottom right-hand corner, filling the foreground and bisecting the middle third on a diagonal. A chunk of cliff bounds the left-hand edge and makes me want to crane my neck, for I am sure that if I could peer around it I would see the cove. The diagonal axis is a foaming mass of dashes and squiggles, a tide moving in; the height of the waves is too exaggerated, ominous even, to suggest an ebb. On the upper, seaward side of this diagonal the paper is blank but for that bit of cliff, the offshore rock, and a horizon line. Two huge rocks dominate the foreground. They slant with the direction of the waves, and their outlines and shadows have been inked vigorously, saturating the paper; it would have taken an age to dry, even in a brisk Atlantic wind. Their forms are familiar if rather sharper here than I know them to be. Maybe it is the boldness with which Emma has rendered them, maybe the work of sea-washing and weathering over one-hundred-and-fifty intervening years.

Between the two rocks is a sandy space. It is closed off by the waves, like the recess in my old paralysing dream, but there the similarity ends. The space in Emma's sketch narrows to a corridor along which figures are hurrying from an access point beyond the right-hand corner: there is a way out. The sand is swarming with tiny figures, an inky notation of arms and legs and hats and random marks dwarfed by the rocks and the towering sea.

Trebarwith Strand is busy enough in the early 1870s. In high season people of leisure rub shoulders, metaphorically of course, with those who eke out livings at the edge of the sea. Coal is carted up here at low tide from beached cargo ships and, before the incoming tide floats the vessels for departure, replaced with finished roofing slates from the surrounding quarries. The business of loading largely falls to women, chains of them working quickly, rhythmically, between the donkey cart and the hold of the ship, where the slates are packed tightly in layers of straw or rushes, or moss. The sea and the moon dictate the timing of most things in this intertidal economy; the collection of sand and seaweed, the unloading and loading of ships, the quarrying of high-grade slate from the lower reaches of a cliff are confined to windows of low-tide hours set without regard for human routine or the rhythms of human sleep. And however carefully those hours are observed, things can go wrong in a flash. In 1844 a vessel was wrecked on the Strand as it was being loaded with slate. Unrecorded lives might be lost to missed footings and rip currents, an outcome narrowly averted in Trollope's tale of seaweed gatherers. The piling waves in Emma's sketch evoke this everyday urgency at the shifting margin of land and sea. A drama of human diminutiveness against the sheer impersonal power of the natural world.

At least, you hope it is only the natural world that is doing the diminishing. This composition resonates with me because the rocks are so familiar and so proximate to the cove, and because the waves are breaking with such squiggly zeal – but it also strikes an uncomfortable note. You cannot help wondering whether the ant-like scale of the human subjects may also be dictated by another kind of vantage point. Ensconced on the cliff with Hardy and the picnic things, thoroughly at leisure, Emma is also looking down on the beach in an attitude of social elevation and more than a little touristic self-indulgence. Seaweed gathering is not mentioned amongst the occupations recorded in census returns for these coastal parishes. Emma's composition pits the poorer sort against the elements by making a teeming throng of them. It turns a blinkered, romanticising eye – a day tripper's eye – to the tough realities of these people's lives, to their humanity. There was nothing romantic about scraping or supplementing a living by dragging masses of tangle from the waves – the weight, the cold, the wet, the danger; nothing whatsoever.

One cannot say with certainty that Tom and Emma never ventured up and over the precipitous hill, but nor is there any reason to believe they did. The high headland, the sheer uninviting climb formed a natural end point, as it does today, for visitors and views alike. In 1897 the editor of the *Saturday Review* approached Hardy for a list of the places where, in his experience, the 'Best Scenery' or most pleasing views were to be found. Hardy bristled at the top-ten tone of this request. 'I am unable to reply to your inquiry', he responded, '[a]t any given moment we like best what meets the mood of that moment'. He nevertheless detailed five views in his West Country 'neighbourhood' that 'rarely or never fail to delight beholders'. One of these is the coast between Beeny Cliff and Trebarwith Strand.

Had they got as far as the cove, Emma might have expended no small amount of ink on the cormorants' rock and the pillar, the snail – but the couple's drives to Trebarwith Strand appear to have been just that, outings to the beach. And you want to keep them there, spare them the miserable, unkind decades of in-compatibility that lie ahead. You want to keep them right here, in their early thirties, in an afternoon of 'quiet dreamy passivity' like the one passed at 'Barwith' Strand in *A Pair of Blue Eyes*. Emma sitting sketching in her high-necked dress, her ringlets piled elaborately, Hardy with his books and that shabby coat, in love or believing himself to be. He studies the sea, its immensity, wrestling it quietly into words. From time to time he opens his notebook and jots down, in a rapid hand, things about blue and movement, tonality; quilts and transformations. Later, in his Cornish novel, he will write of the ocean 'moving and heaving like a counterpane upon a restless sleeper' – as it does, exactly, at high tide in this particular place. Of 'blueness deepen[ing] its colour', waves 'metamorphosed into foam'. The cove lies out of sight, unknown, around the corner and a world away.

We knew that it was there – that we were almost there – in those last trips of my father's life. Take this photograph. Shaun and my father are sitting side by side at a picnic table on the low cliff edge, pint glasses in hand. An empty cheese and onion crisps packet is weighted down by my own glass. The sky and the sea are blue as a cliché and the tide is neither high nor low, the waves breaking powerfully: it is a lovely lively day. Shaun is howling with laughter at something my father has said, and my father looks as happy, as in-the-moment, as I have seen him since my mother's death eleven years before. The waves behind them are shared with the cove, metamorphosing into foam.

As for that momentous first drive down the sanding road, half a century later Hardy, now in his eighties, recalled the visit to the quarry at Penpethy in a late poem titled 'Green Slates'. Emma's death had long since released them both from a bitterly endur-ing marriage and inspired the exquisite, unbearable elegies of

1912–13; it was longer still since Hardy had turned his back on fiction writing and devoted himself to poetry.

'It happened once', the speaker begins, that he searched for a place where 'slates of greenish colour' were quarried, fresh and unweathered, like his young green self, by 'the duller / Loomings of life'. And '[I] saw', he continues,

> *In the quarry standing*
> *A form against the slate background there,*
> *Of fairness eye-commanding.*
>
> *And now, though fifty years have flown me,*
> *With all their dreams and duties,*
> *And strange-pipped dice my hand has thrown me,*
> *And dust are all her beauties,*
>
> *Green slates – seen high on roofs, or lower*
> *In waggon, truck, or lorry –*
> *Cry out: 'Our home was where you saw her*
> *Standing in the quarry!'*

The poem, published in 1925, finds tenderness for Emma in elegy that she seems not to have enjoyed in life. Something lost is recaptured in those last four lines and quite literally shouted from the rooftops. What might smack of hyperbole in a different context is simple and poignant here, not to mention a matter of geological fact. However far afield they have been transported, wheresoever the buildings roofed with their distinctive greenishness, howsoever dulled by the elements, these slates speak of a specific place, a slate bed formed from specific mudstone on a specific tectonic occasion – though only someone who has been to Penpethy will hear exactly what they say.

*

Today began strangely, beautifully. I drove Shaun to the station at Bodmin long before dawn. The late-night sky was infinitely deep and strewn with ragged luminous clouds. *Look!* A sort-of rainbow encircled the moon. A fuzzy halo of untold radius, russet on the inner rim then pale, then blue: moonlight refracted by ice. *Look!* On this of all days. The eastern edge of the sky was lightening when I drove back down the road to Port Gaverne, but it was dark enough ahead. A single light bobbed and lurched in the distance. *There's the sea!* I let myself back into the guest house and lay down for a bit. By the time I sat down to breakfast with my father the clouds had cohered into grey.

My father was tired and very cold. There is no stopping the cancer's progression. But we both tucked into our scrambled eggs and lingered over coffee. I told him about the rainbow weather in space. A monkey's birthday, my father said. We ordered a second cafetière, trying to slow the hours down. Today is my father's last day in Cornwall. Nobody has said as much; there is no need.

By instinct, as we set off on the long drive home, I turned off for Trebarwith Strand. One last time. Leaves rained delicately on our way down the sanding road; the trees are turning fast. It is Monday morning, high tide, the hamlet as deserted as it was packed when we came here yesterday with Shaun. The grey waves, their textures and successive advance. When we turned the last corner into the hamlet the ocean was there, right ahead, and I had a fleeting, awful sense that the waves were pressing inland towards us.

We are sitting in the car at the end of the road, the edge of the sea, the waves of the cove, and I feel that my heart is going to break. I've kept the engine running, the heating cranked up. I would do anything in the world to make my father feel warm, but I feel helpless in the face of his devastating illness.

You will bring me back here afterwards, won't you?

Of course, Dad.

We have to leave; as it is we'll hit the rush hour on the M25. Just five more seconds, and another five. Five seconds are nothing in the scheme of a day: they don't even count as time passing. Five more seconds, I think to myself, and then we will go. Just five more, snatched from somewhere outside time. OK, five more. Just five more . . .

But there was no hoodwinking time: the seconds mounted up. Nine months after that October drive down the sanding road, in high summer my father died.

People say that you should open a window following a death. I did, and a seagull mewed in the night. The lights of the south-coast town below, the darkness of the sea beyond. The hospice in which my father died stood just below the hospital on the hill, long since gone, in which I was born.

I took charge of my father's ashes after the funeral; I insisted on that. I collected them on an August afternoon that was vivid and lovely but ran its course at a glassy remove. The waiting room was dim and numbly familiar. The box of tissues and the artificial roses, chintz armchairs: a kind, tactful best effort against desolate odds. The homely double wardrobe doors that concealed a display of coffin finishes. In the past two weeks I had gained a surfeit of unwanted knowledge, but I had no idea what I should be expecting now.

The undertaker appeared with a green cardboard box. I signed a form and picked up the box. It was surprisingly heavy, a new kind of weight. Outside, the golden light weighed heavily too. I stowed the box in the footwell on the passenger's side and took it home to London, and set it in a corner next to the fireplace. My father's ashes stayed there with us, safe, until the time came to take them to the cove. After the unreality of that afternoon the box became part of things, a quiet presence. I would miss it when it was gone.

Shaun once gave my father, who loved peated single malt, a rare bottle from the obsolete Port Ellen distillery; the label was a subtle shade of lavender. My father never quite finished the bottle. He said he was saving the last measure or two for a special occasion, but I doubt that any occasion would have sufficed: what those drops represented as his health failed was possibility. One evening that autumn we drank them on his behalf and then, the bottle emptied, turned upside down and shaken to be absolutely sure, I packed the green box into a rucksack. Tomorrow we would travel to Cornwall and, the day after, make my father's last journey to the cove. Eventually I soaked off the Port Ellen label; I've used it as a bookmark for years now.

It was a strange drive west, alone but for the box in the passenger's footwell. The old lightening and the new heaviness. The Tamar – KERNOW – the window down. The responsibility weighed heavily too, and lest someone break into the car I took the backpack with me whenever I stopped. I carted it around motorway services, a garden centre, Wadebridge, a farm shop, a pub and, when I went to meet Shaun that evening, Bodmin Parkway Station.

The following morning was mild, cloudy with a prospect of sun. We met up with the others and set off from Tregardock on the old way to the cove. Shaun carried my father's ashes, one last service to his friend. Up behind The Mountain, the bracken over with, the cliff path, the wind, the red-brick tower. Something about the tower seemed different: I couldn't put my finger on it. The crumbling corner and the rabbit holes that, when I was young, caused me such concern on their occupants' behalf. Gorse bloomed in bright patches on the common, and auburn cattle grazed across the seaward flank. Shaun was way ahead, striding towards the tumuli; I could see the red backpack flashing as he dipped up and down with the contours of the land.

The cows, a nine-year-old was saying behind me, they were not safe out here – there was no fence – what if one should slip and fall off the cliff? No way, came a chorus of grown-up reassurance, and grown-ups know about these things: out of the question. They'd never be turned out here if it weren't completely safe. And anyway, cattle don't just fall off cliffs. Of course they don't. If one did come close to the edge it would definitely stop in time: cattle are intelligent and sure-footed creatures. I'd heard that one here before, apropos of rabbits, when I was around this child's age.

Shaun was in the valley now, out of sight. I quickened my pace and walked on ahead, pounding along in the salty wind, the gorse, the heather, the special reverberation of the earth beneath my feet. *I's the b'y that builds the boat / And I's the b'y that sails her*: without my father the lines fell flat. I slowed at the tumuli, looking for the spot where my parents had stood in that last photograph, out on the headland, all the Atlantic and the west behind them. I hurried on and there, suddenly – it is always sudden, however eagerly anticipated – deep down and perfectly in focus, was the cove. I was glad to see that the tide was going out, the rocky slope partly exposed, the cormorants' rock emerging from the waves, the head of the snail coming and going: we'd timed it well. Shaun had stopped on the path a little beyond the wreckers' cottage. He was looking into a part of the cove that I could not yet see, and seemed lost in thought. I started stepping, scrabbling down, and when I passed close to the cliff edge I paused and peered over into the turbulence and heard the airy seashell sound of the open sea. I stopped again at the outcrop above the cottage, and then the path took me back across the valley side. Shaun, I now saw, was not lost in thought at all, but staring at something very attentively. I slowed a little, the path here cow-churned and hardened to an ankle-twisting mess. The rest of the cove swung into view. Shaun turned, grimacing, and I followed his gaze back down to the freshly washed rocks.

Oh shit.

Smack bang in the middle of the cove, arranged by the waves with slapstick precision, lay a dead red cow.

It was horrible. I started laughing. I filled Shaun in on the clifftop conversation. The timing, my father's ashes in the backpack.

The others were coming down the valley. Weakly, for our collective credibility lay dashed with the corpse, we assured the child that the cow had had a heart attack before it fell; that it could not possibly have known fear nor suffered when it met its death. I wanted very badly to believe that myself. The poor form was only as big as a cow, but when we emerged from the bottom of the gulley its bloated presence, the matted auburn hair, the unnatural angle of its neck filled the cove and mocked our business there. We picked our way around the furthermost edge, hugging the foot of the cliff, bent on escaping sight of the thing.

When we reached the other side of the slope, I noticed that the sun was out. The receding waves, their idle rhythms and their syncopations. Tangle heaved and dragged and churned; the iodine saltiness of that day would lodge with me forever. And there, each of us in our own way, we let my father's ashes go. A precious undertaking fulfilled: the rest was up to the elements, the wind and the sea. I cannot say what I felt then, but deep inside it all there was calm, and a kind of relief that was shaped like the waves.

Later, as we climbed up away from the cove, I dropped behind. I did not look down until I reached the outcrop above the wreckers' cottage; the dead cow would be out of sight by then for sure. Shaun was waiting for me. He took my hand, and together we watched as waves broke over the rocks and drained. They carried my father's ashes further and wider, out to sea where my mother had gone. A single cormorant, a large male, stood on the uppermost tip of the cormorants' rock. The bird faced west, away from us, and its wings were open, cruciform, to the heaving glittering sea. To the horizon and beyond.

My mother's rainbow, now the dead cow. The planes of my world had tilted ever so slightly. Its edges were not quite as hard and fast as they once had been. They had grown, or so it seemed to me, ever so slightly permeable.

The sun was dropping, the west full of light as we walked back along the cliff path. There was definitely something different about the tower. It seemed brighter – newer – and brought to mind more vividly than ever the red-brick house in which I grew up, the house that my parents built. As we drew level with the building sunlight bounced from the western façade. The dark apertures were vitrified. There were windows in the tower.

*

The archaeologist has his back to the sea. His hands are thrust deep in the pockets of his overcoat, his collar turned up against the aggravating wind, and his face is obscured by a low-set fedora. It's a wonder the thing stays on at all: a fedora is not an obvious choice of headwear on an exposed clifftop at the messy end of winter, but this is 1941 and the archaeologist has an air of seniority over two flat-capped men who are busy with shovels. He hunches with cold and concentration like a celluloid detective in an exhumation scene. It may well be a late afternoon in February, the day darkening though it has never quite been light. That the days are getting longer makes the lightlessness worse: you know where you stand with midwinter. The grey is cold and the cold grey, the wind unrelenting; it literally chills you to the bone. A persistent drizzle presses at the archaeologist's back. Although he is only forty-one years old the damp registers in his joints. He is prone to head colds and to a lugubriousness of spirit that, in a different age, would probably be diagnosed as seasonal affective disorder. Whichever way you look at it, these are shadowy times. The Dunkirk evacuations are a recent memory. There is no prospect of an end to the Blitz. Hitler is planning to invade Russia.

The men are investigating a Bronze Age tumulus or barrow – a burial mound – on the headland to the south of the cove. The very prominence that lent the site to sacredness makes it unconducive to a winter dig; it is, the archaeologist will recall drily, 'an uncomfortable place to work in a gale'. To his left, out of sight but effectively at his feet, the cove keeps its own counsel. On the other side, also beyond the photograph, the common is crawling with vehicles and heavy machinery. The ancient landscape is being transformed, the hedgebanks that defined it razed, their stones heaped up out of the way, the ground's incline levelled. Trucks are delivering bricks and breeze block, concrete, asbestos, fixtures and fittings along a farm track from the hamlet of Treligga. Time is of the essence for the archaeologist. At some distance to his right, more likely than not, a diminutive red-brick tower is already taking shape.

Since Britain began preparing for war early in 1939, tracts of moor and agricultural land across the far south-west have been requisitioned for airfields and military installations. Archaeological remains that have lain beneath the surface for centuries, millennia, are suddenly endangered by the rapid construction work. Under the aegis of the Ministry of Works' Inspectorate of Ancient Monuments, the archaeologist is on a mission to examine and excavate as many sites as possible, especially constellations of probable barrows, before it is too late. Now it is early 1941. A few weeks ago he was despatched to Treligga when a mechanical scraper cut through the largest and southernmost mound on the common. Hasty excavation revealed a Bronze Age funerary structure, and the archaeologist has stayed on to

investigate seven additional mounds on the site. In this land
of slate it is hard to tell, until you have dug below the scrub
and thin topsoil, whether you are dealing with a human resting
place or a mere rocky eruption. Of the seven mounds, three will
turn out to be tumuli and three natural rock formations; the
seventh, 'decapitated' by machinery, will yield no information
whatsoever.

The presence of tumuli on the common has been marked on
Ordnance Survey maps since the first edition of 1883. I do not
remember exactly when I discovered that a tumulus was a burial
site – I was certainly in my early teens, an anxious time – but
with that awareness grew a queasy, guilty unease. Although I
learned that *tumulus* is the Latin word for 'mound', I took it
as read that the pair of slate-lined craters on the headland were
tumuli. They had to be, because they were fashioned structures
in an otherwise lumpy, blurred topography. Who was I to say
that a burial mound could not have a concave top? And as I
reflected, uneasily, I had once fiddled around inside one of those
craters, hunkered down, watched a buzzard, unaware that I
was doing so on an ancient grave. For all of my innocence at
the time I felt retrospectively guilty, culpable of desecration. I
fretted about it not because I imagined any consequences, but
because I had unwittingly been disrespectful to the dead. Graves
were things around which you tiptoed in every sense.

I wonder what goes through the archaeologist's mind when,
after hours and days of digging, sifting, scraping and brushing,
something not unlike Bakelite solidifies into focus, or, as his
men work their way down into a cairn, the lower strata grow
darker and browner with organic matter, textured perhaps with
charred and comminuted bone. The 'brown mush like decaying

raw bone' that he uncovered up near St Juliot, and 'the much de-
cayed remains of an unburnt skeleton – the right haunch bone
alone recognisable'. Some of the remains may well be animal,
but he wants them to be human – for why does an archaeologist
dig if not in the hope of finding, and what is left of a human
body constitutes a significant find.

I wonder whether, in in-between moments, the archaeologist
reflects on the business of digging up the dead, of bagging up
residual bits of people and removing them from where they once
were placed ceremoniously and for perpetuity; of taking them off,
presumably for analysis and attempted reconstruction though
their deconstruction by fire was a final rite; of squirrelling them
away in tins and sundry containers. That it is not necessarily
wrong to dig up the dead does not make it necessarily right.
Most of us, when we take leave of our dead, or contemplate
or plan how others will take leave of us, have a definitive end
point in mind. Maybe it ought not to matter; these are, after all,
no longer people but mortal remains, earth to earth, human to
humus, ashes to ashes and all that. But yet . . .

I think it might be good to be scattered to the winds and the
waves while you are still a living memory. The last tangible bits
of you are made untouchable, gone elsewhere.

The men have dug down through shillet, thin layers of slate
or shale, to reveal a slate cairn enclosed by a ring of white quartz
boulders. The shillet and 'black turfy sod' inside have led the
men deeper, stratum by stratum, to a pit hollowed out from
the bedrock in the slaty 'crannies' of which are cremated bones.
As they work their way still further into the barrow they will
discover, on ledges and in pits and niches, the cremated remains
of several individuals. In one corner of a rocky alcove they will

lift a slate slab to reveal brown earth which 'encompasses and passes beneath the bones', contains charcoal and fragments of reddened stone, and is up to ten-and-a-half inches deep. Extreme heat has calcined or oxidised the bones to an unearthly brilliant white. When they are analysed forty years later they will be identified as the remains of a young woman who, at the time of her death, had all of her teeth, no caries nor abscesses, and owned a bronze pin.

It is the business of archaeology to report back on the human past by unearthing, analysing and interpreting material remains. Measuring, plotting, photographing. Piecing together and extrapolating from fragments, be they of bones, artefacts or settlements. In the field or lab, in the taking and writing-up of notes, archaeology is a meticulous discipline. You expect your archaeologist, up there on the headland in the gales, to gather and record every detail, every flake and splinter of what he finds, with an obsessiveness befitting his calling.

But it doesn't work like that for the archaeologist. Maybe it is because he almost always seems to be under the weather, catching colds. Perhaps he is just overworked – he has taken on a mammoth task, and time is against him – or perhaps he has, as have I, what some would describe as an untidy mind, not to mention an untidy hand. Maybe something else altogether has set the work of this enigmatic man on a course of perpetual entanglement. It doesn't help that one barrow has been severely damaged – but nor does it help that the archaeologist uses a single notebook to record his digs at Treligga and two other locations; the data on barrows within these disparate groups are muddled together, and in any case thin on detail. The archaeologist removes human remains and other finds in bags and tins and cartons the numbers of which do not always correspond to the numbers in his notebook. Any correlation will be compromised further when bags burst in transit and material is rebagged and stored together with miscellaneous empty labelled bags. He takes many excellent photographs of which some, lacking captions, are rather less useful than they might be. Data and samples from our tumulus on the headland are mixed up with those of its near neighbour. There is a pottery fragment that 'may' have been recovered from the former. In the latter the archaeologist finds cup-marked stones (stones imprinted with a concave hollow or ring) and a rock that he designates, for no archaeological nor fathomable reason, an 'offertory' stone – a term that lay, with the Christian church, many centuries in the barrow's future. There is the cremation sample rebagged in 1945 with the following note: 'Sievings (⅑th inch sieve) . . . from paper bag in . . . black box . . . Is this from the central ossuary of Treligga?' Who knows? A human remnant disinterred and sieved, quite literally unearthed and now worse than lost. There is the perpetual burden of describing the 'reddish sandy', 'greyish clayey shillety', 'sandy loose brown', 'medium brown rather clayey' soils; it does your head in. The inevitable corner-cutting when weather conditions are 'as bad as c[an] be' and the light is 'failing fast'. You start to feel that this is less a systematic excavation than a kind of battle with the place.

And after all this, for reasons that he will take to his own grave, the archaeologist will keep the material from his wartime digs to himself. With the exception of a lecture delivered at the end of the war, he will doggedly resist efforts by the Ancient Monuments Inspectorate to gain access to the findings of the digs it commissioned. Time and house moves have, moreover, a dispersive effect on the stuff that we cart with us through our lives, the letters, pebbles, photographic negatives, tins containing whatever will fit into a tin: buttons, broken watches, that old necklace, the name tag of a much-loved dog, the charred and oxidised and disintegrated bits of prehistoric human beings. Labels will fade or be lost altogether, bags perish, cartons go missing. Only in the early 1980s, upon the archaeologist's death, will the National Archives finally and for an undisclosed sum of money wrest boxes of fugitive notes and material from his executors. Forty-odd years after the clifftop digs a patient archaeologist will try, as she writes, to 'put herself' in the 'shoes' of this elusive man. In collaboration with specialist colleagues she will excavate, as it were, the 'sadly inadequate' excavation record, the 'muddled', unlabelled or illegibly labelled finds, and write it all up for publication in a painstaking labour of meta-archaeology. But before the boxes are handed over, their contents will be disturbed one last time, muddled just a little more, by a burglary at the late archaeologist's home.

The archaeologist is struggling. The chill wind is wreaking havoc with his ears, and his sinuses are so congested that he cannot think straight. In his pockets he makes fists of his numb fingers. Everything is damp, his face, his clothes, the muddy earth, the greasy shillet. The two men are easing and lifting their shovels carefully now, haltingly. The trucks and machinery have fallen silent – the light is going – and now the archaeologist hears only the sea below, its distant rumble though it is close, and the tentative shovelling. Down in the cove there sounds a thunderous crack, a loose rock slammed by powerful waves; he hears, without really noticing, that it is getting on for high tide. He squints at a recess that the men are uncovering in the shallow pit, and he knows that the brownish solids within the soil are not of stone, but bone that has been burned at a relatively low temperature. They were placed here three-and-a-half thousand years ago and the recess covered with shillet and turf, the several burials enclosed in turn beneath a cairn of slate slabs, the tumulus earthed over. Like the other barrows on this clifftop it has been diminished by weather and time, absorbed to the landscape: naturalised. And now? A thought crosses the archaeologist's mind. Maybe he has taken on something that ought never to have been begun. Digging around in a place that shows every sign of not wanting to be known. Looking for things that are not his to find. He puts the thought away.

Three-and-a-half millennia ago, give or take a few centuries, a young woman lived around here. Her teeth were good, and she owned a bronze awl or pin that she may have used to fasten her clothing. She probably lived in a settlement over at Treligga, a location set a little way back from the cliffs with strategic visibility and abundant freshwater springs. Her diet would have included a nutritious array of limpets, mussels and other foods from an ocean uncontaminated by microplastics if not devoid of mercury. Her people may have had more reasons than one for siting their monumental barrows so close – even allowing for subsequent millennia of weathering – to the cliff edge. Their prominence on the skyline, from land and sea alike, may have been bound up with identity and with identity's corollary, power. There was, moreover, something about this west-facing point, the ocean and the setting sun, that inspired wonder, reverence for the natural world, the elements, gods of one kind or another, and I know that was so because I sense it here today. It feels like the edge of everything. Then, when the possibility of something beyond the horizon – land, the sphericity of the world – was remote to say the least, it must truly have been the edge of everything. The gales pummelling their own airy element.

But how the young woman experienced this spot is anybody's guess. Maybe it was off limits, a sacred place fluttering with spirits of the dead, maybe not. Maybe she saw a rainbow here; I hope she did. If so it would have been a thing of sheer wonder, sent from her god or gods as it was for those whose stories eventually coalesced in the Book of Genesis. What must it have been like to see a rainbow through her eyes?

As for the cove, who knows. It would have been a cove of sorts, but not one that I would recognise. Where today there are angles and sliced façades, the gulley, space and jumbled rocks, there may have been a considerable volume of slate. The stream that rushes down through the gulley would, back then, have flowed over bedrock where now there is air, before falling over into the sea.

*

Livestock has been falling off Cornish cliffs since time immemorial. John Norden noted four centuries ago that sheep at Tintagel sometimes fell 'headlonge into the sea'. But the dead red cow haunted me because it was so immediate and because it smacked of one coincidence too many. The first, the rainbow rising from the cove at that moment of all moments, was surely down to changeable weather, to sun shining at a certain angle into rain: a wonderful thing (rainbows are always wonderful), and a scientifically basic one. And yet. The second was clearly attributable to the misplaced footing of a hapless ruminant. And yet. I could not quite shake a shadowy sense that, taken together, their timing was significant. Maybe it was me. And yet.

Until my mother's death and what transpired afterwards, I had not really experienced anything that I would describe as uncanny, let alone out-and-out supernatural. Peer pressure not-withstanding, I do not think I ever believed in ghosts when I was a child, certainly not in the conventional sense of apparitions and not in any felt way that I can recall. My parents were unam-biguous when it came to the supernatural, and I willingly took my lead from them: there was reason enough for worry in this world as it was, what with Stranger Danger, and my unspeakable knowledge that the tide would cut us off when we next went to Cornwall, and the possibility that my parents could die. Not to mention what Mr Thoroughgood, who wore Jesus sandals, told us in assembly about thinking a thing being as bad as saying it. That really freaked me out, though his theological point rather passed me by; I was more than capable of finding myself guilty without the help of an omniscient god. For a while just having thoughts was a worrying thing to do.

The obscure interior of a derelict house at the bottom of the lane unnerved me in ways that did not need to be analysed: it was enough to push through giant feral rhododendrons, amongst which I felt a little too alone – or was it that I might not be alone? – and peer through a broken pane into the shadows and, beyond the shadows, dark. Talk of ghosts, on the other hand, was an abstract and routine playground theme. One of my classmates, a popular individual who maintained her standing by telling sensational lies, claimed to have seen generic ghosts such as headless horsemen and see-through monks; even my disastrous gullibility stopped well short of that. Rather more intriguing was my then-best friend's disclosure that her mother saw and felt unspecified Things. What kinds of things? Just Things, she sees and feels Things. But what? Things. Stuff.

It was around this time, in my last year at primary school, that I encountered Walter de la Mare's exquisite poem 'The Listeners'. Mrs G, as I came to call her, read it to us on a frost-bright winter day. Mrs G taught us on Tuesdays and Thursdays, and I adored her. She told my mother that she'd grown up next door to the Kray twins, on Vallance Road in Bethnal Green, not that I knew who the Krays were back then. She called a spade a spade and then some, and led us into stories and poems with a fizzing sense of adventure, of the wonders contained in words. I remember the clarity of that morning, how everything in it had heightened definition. '"Is there anybody there?" said the Traveller, / Knocking on the moonlit door . . .' – and when Mrs G had finished I put up my hand and asked her to read it all over again.

We know nothing about the Traveller, only that his eyes are grey and that he has come or returned here in fulfilment of some past promise. He knocks again, harder, and still no one answers:

> But only a host of phantom listeners
>   That dwelt in the lone house then
> Stood listening in the quiet of the moonlight
>   To that voice from the world of men . . .

I found these lines unbearably sad and still do, decades after I first heard them, well over a century after they were penned. What the poem was 'about' eluded me; the listeners seemed somehow less than ghosts – which, I'd reflect when I was much older, is perhaps to say that they were more. I sensed, in ways that I could not then articulate, that 'The Listeners' was concerned with loneliness. With separation: the man in his world and the phantom listeners in theirs, aware of one another but held apart by some dimensional divide, a kind of mutual ghostliness. The listeners listen to his voice; he feels 'their strangeness' in his heart, their 'stillness answering his cry'. Are they 'phantom', I wonder now, in a rather more mundane sense: imagined, felt into being by the 'one man left awake', left behind in his world? As if their phantom existence consists in listening, which is to say bearing witness, to his presence – to his very being. Or is the Traveller in his world of men a ghost to the listeners in theirs? Is he ghostly because he has come too late, because his business is unfinishable? This is not a ghost poem, but a poem that invites you to think about whether, and what, and how a ghost might be. Whether the fact that you don't subscribe to the possible existence of other worlds, dimensions, energies, call them what you will, or at least insist that you do not, means that there are or can be no such Things. It doesn't, for no one can prove a negative.

When I got home from school on that winter day, I rifled through my parents' bookshelves and found 'The Listeners' in *An Anthology of Modern Verse*, rather less modern inside and out than it used to be. I appropriated the musty, battered volume – it was published in the 1920s and dedicated to Thomas Hardy, 'Greatest of the Moderns' – and for many months kept it on my bedside table with a bookmark at page 57. I read 'The Listeners' over and over again, and the enigmatic lines, their what-if-ness, wove themselves into the fabric of my life.

Life moves on and you move on to other things; you grow up, and instead of the purpose-made bookmarks that you used punctiliously when you were a child you mark places with dried leaves and Christmas gift tags, restaurant cards, the label from a special bottle. But although you haven't given them a thought in years the listeners are there. The poem will come to mind one day, word for word across the intervening years and with renewed resonance; poetry encountered in childhood has a knack of doing that. Maybe it has to do with those two worlds or realities, each inaccessible, ghostly to the other yet also some-how mutually sensed – heartfelt, heard – and they have become relevant to the negotiations with absence that constitute grief. Maybe it is that ghostly curse of unresolvable business. Maybe it is age, that you have become one of those people who say they know less the longer they live – not that what you know is nec-essarily diminishing (though you do forget names from time to time), but that you are ever more conscious of the scale of what you don't and will never know, and of what cannot be known. Maybe some change in your inner weather has summoned up the lines, rather as an affecting dream may disappear beyond recall when you wake, yet turn up months, years later in vivid detail and a mood that feels both strange and strangely familiar.

As for Mrs G, we exchanged Christmas cards in the year that I left primary school, and before I knew it we were writing to each other regularly though we only lived two miles apart. I've no idea whether she knew of the trauma that was my secondary education; there must have been plenty to read between the lines.

Mrs G was the only person I have ever known with handwriting more unpredictable and less legible than mine. Reading back through her side of our correspondence today I am struck afresh, as I appreciated then, that she wrote to my eleven-year-old self as to an adult peer, though her letters admittedly became more subversive as I got older. I was in the sixth form when she mentioned that her right foot was numb. Her vigorous, chaotic handwriting grew quieter, newly wayward, and one day she wrote with terrible news of a diagnosis: motor neurone disease. In my first weeks at university she wrote frequently, cheering me on though the letters grew brief, and by Christmas they had stopped altogether. I visited in the holidays of that first academic year and typed up cheerful letters to friends that she dictated against the mounting odds. The double remove of dictation and type dulled her exuberant written voice. Then she did not have breath to dictate her letters either and then, when I was almost nineteen and she forty-six, Mrs G died. I miss her friendship after all these years, her wisdom and her wickedness. And had she lived I think there would eventually have been a wide-ranging epistolary debate about the Traveller and the listeners. As it is, the poem is forever inflected with her cockney accent and incomparable feel for the poem's spoken voice – its rhythms and its cadences –

And how the silence surged softly backward,
When the plunging hoofs were gone.

*

The Atlantic was pure light when, as my father's ashes drifted away, I stood with Shaun on the promontory above the cove and watched the lone cormorant watching the sea. There was something more than cruciform about the craggy silhouette. The bird's wings outstretched as though embracing immensity. *This,* it seemed to say. *The light. The ocean. All of it.* Waves gathered themselves, and broke. The sun deepening in the west. I knew that my cove would never be the same again. Of course it would not, because my parents were gone. And because of something else that I could no more explain than dismiss. Coincidences happen, but.

Maybe, as I said before, it was just me. Grief can predispose you to see things. It makes you apt to find significance in happenings, however inconsequential or accidental they may appear to others. It sensitises you to timings and wherefores, and therefores. If something is significant it means that you are in receipt of a sign. It means that connection is not lost.

Some months later, when my thoughts were roaming through the small hours, I saw the sea glinting, its colour beyond colour. The water heaved quietly, rhythmically, and then somehow I was down in the cove and the rocks stretched away as though the tide had gone far out, further and further, never to return. The wrapping, towering cliffs at my back: I sensed them as I looked out into the light, and I heard the cove's special contained atmosphere, which was less a sound than a way of making things sound. *But only a host of phantom listeners . . .* That is when, approaching sleep at last, I noticed the line. It came from a place more than thirty years deep and its rhythms found their old footholds in my mind; the poem followed, bit by bit.

The phantom listeners lent words to a feeling I was starting to have about the cove. It was nothing specific, certainly nothing to which you would apply the term 'ghost'. Their self-contained presence – *listening . . . [t]o that voice from the world of men* – chimed with a fugitive sense that there was more to the cove than I could see, something in the nature of the place, worlds brushing or bumping against one another.

One thing was clear. The cove, the place in which, throughout my childhood and teens, I had felt happiest, and safe; that, excepting the dark caves on the southern side, I knew inside out, was getting complicated. Griefs were laid up in its slate strata. Strange things had been happening here. I felt a twinge of apprehension when Shaun and I next passed the tumuli. The best part of a year had elapsed since we came this way with my father's ashes. Who knew what I was going find when we came over the valley brow, what might have happened at the cove, what might happen while we were there. Whether my cove would be there at all. I followed Shaun slowly down the first short zig of the zigzag path. And there, below, was the cove like a picture of itself: the sea postcard-blue, the shapes revealed, the snail, the pillar, the cormorants' rock. Hello cove, I heard myself say. I hurried on down. The gulley was slimy underfoot, the stream running wide, but my feet remembered what to do. Out into the light, the cove. The echoing and the seaweed freshness. I knew that I was back.

Later, on the low-tide rocks, I looked into bodies of water that were not quite sea nor yet quite pool and eddied, and seeped into one another. A distinctive agitation caught my eye, an effect too localised, too deliberate, to be caused by currents or the skimming wind, and I saw that a starfish was stirring in the opalescent depth.

*

You are on your hands and knees now, peering through your reflection to the bottom of the almost-pool. The water threaded with filigree light, a leisurely sloshing of sea at your back. You have never seen a living starfish before, though you've encountered plenty of dead ones washed up on beaches or displayed on people's bathroom windowsills, and you have read about them in your books on seashore life. This individual is pale gold, with symmetrical configurations of stubby whitish spines. When it lifts one of its bendy limbs you can see that the underside is furnished with tube feet that look a bit like suckers and are tinged with pink. The starfish inches across the slate bottom. Its levering, gliding action is strangely redolent of walking but is in fact a unique form of hydraulic locomotion. This sophisticated, brainless echinoderm has a circulatory system of tubes that run not with blood but with seawater; their ends, those tube feet, are made to expand or contract by means of a valve that controls the creature's internal water pressure. You watch as a flexible arm begins to investigate a clump of mussels. It touches them lightly, lingeringly, and then it withdraws, and reaches out again and feels further, lingering longer.

Starfish bypass the whole business of eating: they digest their prey in its own shell. Those pink pressurised tube feet will force the two halves of a mussel shell fractionally apart. The starfish will then evert its stomach through the tiny crack, releasing digestive juices to break down the mussel's flesh. Once the shell's inhabitant is sufficiently digested the stomach will be retracted along with what remains of the nutritious gloop. Thankfully mussels also lack brains, though they certainly have nerves. What must it be like to be digested? you wonder in passing, and wish you hadn't.

The more you learn about starfish, the stranger and more wonderful these creatures become. Science fiction would be hard-pressed to surpass the design of this animal with attributes exceeding the creaturely – with hydraulic mechanics at one extreme and, at the other, a faintly plant-like capacity to regrow amputated limbs. Its exquisite, self-regenerating symmetry and the forceful, seeping efficiency of its feeding habits. The unthinking purposefulness, the sheer otherness.

You are suddenly and acutely conscious that you know very little about the world. A second spiny arm extends over the mussels and is drawn back rather, but not quite, like a finger testing for dust. You wonder how the starfish experiences touch. You think of the ocean coursing through the creature's not-quite veins.

*

The following spring, towards the end of an early-April afternoon, Shaun and I sat on the slaty ledge sequestered from the land, the ocean before us, the tide charging in at our feet. Sun flooded from the west and made me feel golden, warmer than I was. I did not want to be anywhere in the world but right there and right then, with Shaun.

The rocks were submerging rapidly: sea heaved over the composite form of the snail and rose around the cormorants' rock. Two birds perched on top, their wings folded, their snaky forms attentive. I did not, I said, recall the tide coming in so fast, though I often think or say that when I've been away from the cove for a while. A new note sounded in the agitation, a thud that, considered alone, I would never attribute to water. The traces of our low-tide hours were underwater as the rocks were, not that we had left much behind, a few footprints in the finest shingle, two thrift blooms picked from the headland and tucked into a special spot. I watched waves pile into spaces where I had jumped across the rocks, soaked up the sun, breathed in the seaweed air, pocketed a pebble. In a place like the cove you are always a little ephemeral.

The horizon line. My parents' ashes. Particles sinking down through years to the bottom of the sea or coming and going in water that pitched and towered like canyons, edifices, cliffs. I pictured open ocean and maybe, just maybe, a pale speck embedded in a wave.

My thoughts wandered on due west from the cove, the crests and the troughs, the bright horizon keeping pace. On towards Newfoundland, the terrible seas, the granite and the wilderness, the pockets and edges of human endeavour – *I's the b'y that builds the boat / And I's the b'y that sails her* – on across the Gulf of St Lawrence, on into the vastness of Canada, on and on to that prairie sea where churches set sail and where Shaun is from. Fifty degrees north, give or take: the latitudinal axis of my life.

My fingers chanced on two distinctive edges. As I sat and looked out to sea one hand had been rummaging amongst the scattered bits of slate. My fingertips knew a right angle when they felt it. I picked the piece up and inspected it. It was flat, roughly a centimetre and a half thick, and formed a chunky L around that crisp right angle. Although the outer corners just exceeded or just fell short of ninety degrees, the lines brought the constructed silhouette of the clifftop church to mind.

The cove was a quarry, I said.

One side of the slate was scored with straight hairlines, as if it had been marked up or worked with a tool. The edges were ridged – foliated – and the layers had begun to split apart under some geological or, I now saw, mechanical stress.

Of course it was a quarry, Shaun replied, I always knew that.

You've known that all this time and you never said?

How on earth could you not have known? Look around you. Look at the place.

How on earth could I not have known? Because. I was well aware that the dramatic coast around Tintagel had been shaped in no small measure by slate quarrying; it was the subject of a National Trust interpretation board at Trebarwith Strand. Even were I not, how else might you account for the cove's unique angularities, the gulley and its sheer walls, the cuboid pillar, the oblong recesses, and for the gazillion fragments of slate littering these edges of the land? I didn't know; it had never occurred to me to wonder about them. The valley and the cove were what they were, the valley and the cove.

I am holding that piece of slate now, at my desk in Northamptonshire. The pale surface changes with the light, but its colour is somewhere between green and grey and the edges are crusty with red and ochre, oxide tints. Seen from above, flat on my desk, the slate is matte like cardboard, but if I tilt it towards the window on this overcast Midland day it reflects the light like satin. To the touch it is somewhere between those two materials, a texture all of its own. If I were to work one of my father's old wood chisels into a fissure between the layers I might chip and prise the upper leaf away and make the slate thinner and flatter still, thin as a finished roofing slate.

That the cove was once a quarry was, it turned out, self-evident to just about everyone but me. That my parents knew is put beyond doubt by an image that didn't make the cut for the family slide show, but was never thrown away; I chanced upon it fairly recently in a box of mildewed discards. My father took the photograph in the very early seventies from a viewpoint on the precipitous slope just above the stream. A ball of thrift – a nice detail; my father was a perfectionist – blooms in the foreground, and the eye is led over the top of the gulley to the rocks of the cove beyond. It's a lovely sunny day, and half a century of storage in various lofts has barely touched the sea's bright blue. That early memory, vivid as a snapshot and almost as brief: *I's the by that bys the by.* Bumping down through the dark gulley on my father's shoulders, the sky bright and – as I was too small to notice, let alone commit to memory, but see now in this discarded photograph – three rusted iron rails traversing the gulley overhead. Two or three years later they were gone, along with who knows what other residual bits of hardware and infrastructure. As for the internet, when I got around to Googling the cove, seven of the first ten results would describe the place as a former quarry. And it's reasonable to assume a commensurate degree of awareness in the pre-internet age, for as the 1990s receded to the eighties, seventies, sixties, fifties, coastal slate quarrying was a living memory. Not to mention the Ordnance Survey's numerous maps that show scatterings of quarries – largely and, in later versions, entirely disused – in the environs of the cove.

What is common knowledge tends not to be discussed be-cause it is common knowledge. The cove's manifest history was part of the fabric of things. I never saw those quarry graphics because I never looked for the cove on a map: I knew the way, and even when Shaun bought that first Ordnance Survey I only really paid attention to Trebarwith Strand. When we found our way from Tintagel, past the old quarries, the hacked and blasted cliffs, the waves' end-on solidity, Tennyson's scullock, I did not make any connection between what I read about quarrying on the interpretation board and the cove – my cove – just around the headland. The bottom line is that I was incurious. Curiosity is predicated on not knowing – or rather, on knowing that you do not know. Had I wondered aloud about the ruins and the strange angular rocks, someone would have enlightened me on the spot. How on earth could I not have known? Because I knew the cove too well, in my own way: I was deeply involved with it long before I had any idea of what a quarry was. The quarry stuff was literally over my head.

In the seconds that it took me to pick up that angular bit of slate, little enough happened on the surface of things. Waves advanced and bumped against rock, seagulls wheeled. As far as the world was concerned the cove remained the same – insofar as a place of tides and running streams and endlessly eroding cliffs can ever be quite the same from one moment to the next – yet it had metamorphosed in my fingers, before my very eyes. I'd known and loved this place for my entire life, almost fifty years, and in that instant I discovered that I barely knew it at all. The sloping cliff bases, the sliced faces, the shapes of the rocks: everything was so familiar, and suddenly so new.

Of course it was a quarry.

It was blindingly obvious, but the realisation astounded me. The ruins and tracks around the cove were one thing – the wreckers' cottage, the villa, the mysterious sheep tunnel – but the cove itself another. Not only was my wild cove shaped by men, it was, I saw there and then, my fingers tracing those edges, that angle, worked, gouged, disembowelled to a very considerable extent. Why did this matter? It was only a fact. I didn't know: it mattered because, and it mattered very much. Perhaps it was a little like having a friend and discovering one day, after many years, that they are not the person you have known but another person altogether. I felt stupid, too, wrapped for half a century in my special ignorance.

I pocketed the piece of slate. The horizon had dissolved to milkiness and the open ocean glinted orange on bronze. I could not name the colour of the churning water at our feet: it was blue and grey and green and black and none of these. We got to our feet and shrugged on our backpacks, and waited to leave. A pure, intense seaweed smell came and vanished. We can go now, I said.

The sea heaved and fell and heaved, and threw itself at the cut rockfaces insistently, indifferently. The cove had been shaped by human hands in ways that I'd barely begun to appreciate, but it was no less wild for that.

*

The fog showed every intention of sticking around. It was there at the windows of the guest house when Shaun and I got up, Boscastle engulfed. It was still there after breakfast, massy and clammy, when we set off in the car for Tregardock. We stopped at a garage from which, all other things being equal, you could look across an undeveloped plot and straight up to Rough Tor as you pumped the petrol. Even now, in the blank beyond, I thought I could see the crags of the tor taking shape; the world might have been a sheet of bromide floating in a developing tray. Norden thought the tors of Bodmin moor 'so crowned with mightie rockes' resembling 'toweres, howses, chimnies, and such like' that you might, from afar, 'suppose them to be greate Cyties planted on the hills'. *Mightie rockes*, I thought; castles in the air. They lacked substance today, but as the pump whirred and the petrol fumed its agreeable smell the tor's bulk made a light shadow in the lighter grey.

I went inside to pay. I recognised the bespectacled man who was sorting newspapers at the counter. Behind him a picture window gave onto the forecourt and Rough Tor beyond. I said that I thought it a shame things were not arranged such that he could enjoy the view. There wasn't exactly anything to see today was there, he replied. Fair enough. But I'd been coming here for years; the till had always faced away from the window. How could he bear to have that view of Rough Tor at his back? On a clear day, of course . . . it wouldn't be the same from one minute to the next what with the light, the Atlantic weather . . . sometimes you must reach out from here and almost touch the rocks . . . The man removed his glasses and looked at me severely. The tor was always there, he said, wasn't it.

Fog alters the sound of a car engine even when you are inside and the windows are closed. I do not know if this is objectively the case, or whether it happens because the world is visually muted, made mysterious. Shapes imply themselves and dissipate, or come upon you suddenly and vividly. Hazy volumes rushed at the windscreen as we drove deep through lanes in the direction of the sea. The hedgebanks pressed in towards us too, soft grass weighed down with sogginess, the flaming shapes of hart's tongue ferns. Alexanders, greenish umbelliferous globes, and the several pinks of campion: shocking, salmon, rose. The drawn-out screech of bramble on bodywork as we eased around a hairpin bend. There was a special starkness to the thorn trees in their greyed-out surroundings, and something about them – a pagan twigginess perhaps, or the way they heaved into focus, or their wind-blown shapes, the shape of movement – could make you think them silently animate. Through a gateway I saw the fog barrelling across a field. It moved just above ground level, as apparitions are meant to do, and in the narrow stratum of clarity grass stretched off into three dimensions. Fog can travel at surprising speed, especially when it is sent from the sea.

We parked at Tregardock. The farmyard was hushed. I do not remember when the pigs disappeared, only that one day there were none and the farm did not smell and sound so much like a place where animals lived, and over time the buildings were smartened up and windows appeared in the barns and the pigsty.

As we set off down the track nothing was audible besides our footsteps and manifold sounds of moisture. We trod softly, self-conscious in our muffled, enchanted little world beyond which, if the senses were to be believed, lay nothing. Springs trickled barely behind the scenes. A drip-dripping from overhanging branches and the high green saturated banks. Moss, ivy, hart's tongues, navelworts. Tiny showers broke out when the kissing gate swung back against its slate surround. The springs emerged as fluent streams. Stitchwort, celandines: the season growing.

Out into the open, if that is the right word for space of such apparent density; sharp left and down amongst the blackthorns, down into the valley. The fog driving into our faces softly, steadily. Its vertical phases, thorn trees looming and fading, a blank homogeneity beyond. The slaty path glistened and was greasy

underfoot; I slipped once and almost fell. The thorns were stud-
ded with fat cream buds, starry in places with the first white
blossoms. Drops lined up along the undersides of their leafless
branches and elongated with gravity, and fell. The branches
and rapier spines of blackthorn are anything but black: they are
brownish purples tapering to russets and mahoganies and, at
dusk or in the muted atmosphere of a day like this, silverish.
A single flower caught my eye: its stamens clutched a nugget
of moisture as if entrusted with a precious stone. The drop was
crystalline as the day was not, and the dull light was somehow
gathered into it and reflected back brilliantly. Blackthorn in fog,
I thought, fog in blackthorn.

When we came out on the clifftop a rolling mass enveloped
us. We debated briefly whether to turn back. Beads of fog
were strung through gorse, threaded on gossamer and tangled
red dodder. The sea sounded far below, a sleepy intermittent
heave.

Something else was on the air, not sound so much as an idea
of sound. Maybe I heard it because I knew the foghorn would
be blasting at Trevose Head, miles to the south. I remember
climbing up inside the lighthouse when I was small and the
place was still manned: it was a sunny day, and I suspect the
Fresnel lenses were rotating for our benefit. I thought they were
the most marvellous things I had ever seen, their dynamic pat-
terns and the way they made rainbow pieces of the light.

If you could climb to the top floor of the brick tower and
knew exactly where to look, and assuming of course that the
night were clear, surely you would glimpse the lighthouse, its
rhythmic sweep telescoped to a distant wink. There was no sign
of the tower today.

You could have heard a pin drop on the common. There is nothing like an Atlantic fog – real fog, not the swirling mystical stuff of Camelot – to make familiar territory strange. Shapes came and went. A contour of the cliff. A sudden munching close at hand, and corporeal shades of cows. A slaty lump came to life when we passed an outcrop on the headland. The peregrine stirred powerfully, gathering itself, and lifted off across our path – the bandit face, the barred underside – and then it was a swift shadow, then was gone.

A single shot rang out below, the sea cracking.

As we descended the valley the fog became cloud. Just beyond the wreckers' cottage a slice of the world reappeared in all its colours and perspective, fully formed beneath the fallen-in sky. The rocks were wet on this dripping day, but we'd checked the times and I knew the tide would be going out. The stream flowed wide across the slate. I kept on walking towards the gulley. We're not going down today, Shaun said, it's dangerous. I am, I said. No you're not. You'll fall and hurt yourself. He turned and headed up the bank. I took another step, and another, facet by tilting slippery facet, the brown slime and the trickling walls, the miniature ferns, a childish frisson of disobedience.

My feet had been doing this for decades. But as they smacked on the film of water, feeling their way into recesses, leaning into each upper edge, it was as though I saw the gulley for the first time. The straight walls, the angles and planes could not but have been shaped with tools. You couldn't think otherwise, not that I had: until recently I had not given the matter any thought at all.

On wave-worn rock at the very end I fell and scraped an elbow. I hoped Shaun hadn't noticed. I slipped further, pitched feet first over the edge and, which was rather neat, landed standing in the cove. The air was salt and damp, faintly muddy, and the cove was lit with an eerie brightness that did not come from the presumed direction of the sun but was immanent in the fog.

I saw that the cliff at the further corner formed a right angle. That the ledge at the back of the fishy cave had a certain regularity though high tides upon high tides had softened its edges. I stepped in the widest watery spaces amongst the first rocks. Those accumulations of thin slates like After Eights: of course they had been split and cut by more than natural forces. That nub of rusted iron embedded in rock. The rhombus, its damp lustre: I now inferred that those distinctive edges had been cut or sawn. Everywhere I looked, it seemed, was the work of men. A rounded rock with an angular gouge, and a flat one striated with parallel grooves. An undulating rock scored with near-circles: these carvings smacked less of quarrying than of the pagan, but that must be par for the course in a land of clootie wells and Merliniana. I leapt to conclusions with the zeal of the newly enlightened, and saw human doings everywhere in the cove.

Water was soaking into my hiking boots. I climbed onto my usual rock in the spreading stream, and looked out to sea. The waves heaved in the aperture, sloshing like vertigo, and as they pulled back I saw that the channel had straight sides and must have been cut; how else, in this treacherous place, might boats have come to moor at that rusted ring in the cliff face to my left? The cove became ever stranger as I recognised, or thought I did, the artifice of it all. Or perhaps it was I who had become a stranger in my cove. Balanced on my lump of yellowing quartz, I felt suddenly and acutely self-conscious – as if I were trespassing or being observed, or listened to. The weather amplified it all, the ghostly light, the contracted world. The pale veined rock made me think of an unhoused, vulnerable brain. It is true that, one day, standing on this rock, I would nearly lose my life and be petrified, turned momentarily by fear to stone.

A dark expanse unfolded beyond the rocks: the fog was lifting at a rate of knots. I picked my way back up through the gulley, and jumped across the stream, and scrambled up a slate-loose bank and went to look for Shaun. I found him perched on the low cliff at the edge of the villa foundation. You were watching over me. Of course I was, he said.

The valley side was tinted with squills. Their outer parts were a shade of lilac and their anthers cobalt, their fleshy leaves curled like fine wood shavings, their element the sea-sodden air. Spring squills live between land and sea, like the lovely mini-ature maritime ferns that thrive in the gulley's salt atmosphere. These are plants after my heart, what with their terrestrial roots and their exceptional tolerance of sea spray on their foliage – on their skin, I want to say.

By the time we reached the headland the tower had reap-peared. Thumping back across the common I scrutinised each rocky eruption for a still, watchful form – but I knew that the peregrine was not to be looked for, that it had shown itself to us by chance, or grace. As we passed the tower, it occurred to me that something else had changed. The brick planes and edges seemed too uniform: they formed a perfect cuboid. To my mind the structure was slightly irregular: I could have sworn that some kind of walled staircase grew from one side. Maybe it was me. The tower had been away, after all, and everything looks bright and pristine when revealed after fog. I dawdled on the way back to the farm. Towards the top of the track I caught a fleeting smell of pigs – not the putrid stench of manure spread on land, but the brisker pungency of living animals.

As we drove away through the drenched lanes, I thought about the pigsty in which no pigs had lived for many years: how it was inhabited these days by holidaymakers, a patio and picnic table where once there was mud for wallowing, and how very odd it was that I had smelled that smell. I thought about a time, long ago now, when Shaun and I had met a herd of piglets stampeding down the track, how they had milled and squealed around our legs, their distinctive smell and their picture-book tails, and how we had laughed and laughed, the exhilaration of it all. About the many times in my childhood when my father drove us down to Tregardock, the blue V – *there's the sea! I can see the sea!* – and parked tight against the bank, and I could barely wait to be released from the car and run ahead to visit the pigs. The sows paid little attention to me – they grunted and snuffled about as if conversing with themselves, minding their own foraging business – but the piglets were new to the world, brimming with interest, and always came running. I missed the pigs.

We turned onto the coast road, and Rough Tor was inky in the fog's aftermath.

*

I'd known the contours of the valley and the cove in my own unquestioning way, and now, having picked up that angled piece of slate, I wanted to know about them; I wanted facts. After a lifetime of indifference I was suddenly ravenous for maps: I wanted to lay my hands on every edition of every sheet on which the cove was marked. And local histories, and archaeo-logical reports. I would contact the National Trust. Maybe local farmers would talk to me. I would find out about the tower, how it came to be there, and who, after all this time, had given it windows. I'd scramble around the valley, the cove, its edges, to all appearances as I had always done – except that I would now be looking for information. Quite what I hoped to do with it when I found it was about as clear as fog.

Back at home I set the slate on my desk and hit the inter-net. That the cove is a former quarry was the tip of the iceberg. I was informed repeatedly that the cove is also haunted: not just haunted, *very* haunted. Twenty years previously I'd have dismissed that out of hand. Of course it is, I thought now with a metaphorical shrug, I could have told you that. And anyway, setting aside the odd strange happening, an uncanny whiff or two, *I* haunt the cove: *I* come back to it time and again. As I read on, however, the specifics proved wearisomely off-the-shelf, spirits of drowned fishermen and shipwreck victims, as you might expect, not to mention the remorseful ghost of a man who, according to an archetypal tale of sibling rivalry, set fire to the family farm in the valley only to learn that he'd inherited it. I thought the cove was more haunted than that, and in ways that could not be attributed nor personified. Haunted, haunting. A passing reference sent me off to my local university library, where I ordered up the *International Directory of Haunted Places* – it was published by Penguin and therefore had to be credible – and found the cove listed, according to unspecified criteria, amongst the seven hundred most haunted places in the world. *Wow.* The cove, I read, was haunted by 'many unidentified presences', and that phrase resonated with me: that was it, exactly. But shipwrecked sailors and the remorseful sibling ensued, and with those – and the following entry, concerning 'a phantom coach with four horses and a headless coachman' – the *Directory* lost me; I'd heard those sorts of thing in the playground ages ago. It was more complex and less quantifiable than that, something in the nature of the place, its place-memory.

I went back to fact-finding. I worked my way through a great deal of geology, most of which was lost on me, and beyond the fact that the cove had been quarried I was none the wiser as to the practicalities thereof – how it was shaped, frequented, occupied, how it came to be. Coastal extraction is, after all, a footnote in the history of quarrying. I spoke to someone at the National Trust, who could offer no further information on the subject but mentioned that the valley was owned privately. Somebody actually owned my cove! *My* cove: that was a new, slightly tricky idea. I continued trawling online library catalogues, made a few phone calls, and at last, thanks to a wonderful lady at County Hall in Truro, found myself printing out the PDF of an archaeological report titled *Coastal Slate Quarries: Tintagel to Trebarwith.* Its scope clearly stopped short of the cove, but it would surely go some way towards telling me how my cove had come into being.

The document mapped and inventoried each quarry on that stretch of coast and was written in a language that, though it was English, I didn't understand. I ploughed through the pages, trying to reconcile their eye-watering detail with the turbulent overgrown cliffs. I'd struggled to find any facts at all, and now I had too many. I didn't know what to do with the report, but I leafed through it from time to time and slowly, incidental-ly, I picked up a vocabulary of box caves and splitting sheds;

whims and strong points and poppet heads. One day, on the path to Tintagel above the chaos and the strange monumental forms, I spotted a section of curzeyway in a bramble thicket. The wall curved slightly, enclosing and retaining what remained of a raised platform. A donkey whim! I said triumphantly, and told Shaun about the animals that laboured around the whim or winding gear, blindfold against dizziness, hauling two-ton blocks of slate up the cliff above Trebarwith Strand.

The report, for all of its detail, had interesting limitations. What remains of each quarry is plotted painstakingly, each accessible element described – yet the author cautions that, when all is said and done, the precise practicalities of extracting slate from the cliff face remain conjectural. The geological complexity that made coastal quarrying a worthwhile enterprise also made it a thoroughly opportunistic one. Sites and methods shifted with the character and quality of the slate, and of course as the cliff itself was quarried away. The extant parts may be plotted like dots but will not, should you attempt to join them, form a comprehensive picture.

Another document arrived from Truro. This one was a survey of the so-called historic environment – the physical traces of past human activity – in a series of farms on the North Cornwall coast including, of all places, Trebarwith. It was exactly the kind of material I craved, in a depth that I had not imagined possible: a field-by-field description of the land from which the cove was carved. And this too was problematic. Not only did somebody appear to own my cove, it unsettled me, at a wholly unreasonable but very real level, that someone else had acquainted themselves so minutely with the place. It was as if, on a brilliant day when the blue sky and the towering slate had special intensity, I had made my way down beside the stream and out across the low-tide rocks, one leap after another, and splashed on around the slope and, finding the sea withdrawn to a dreamlike lapping calm, had trodden on, barefoot now, over slate, and paddled through the further shallows, the luminous water and moon jellyfish, and discovered, ensconced amongst the rocks in the brightest depths of my cove, a stranger swigging from a can of Coke or finishing an apple.

This section of the second report made for strange reading. At my desk nearly three hundred miles away I recognised just about every earthwork, ruin and structure detailed therein; some, like the wreckers' cottage and the villa, and of course the ledge, I had haunted since I was small. They changed constantly and always had done, what with slates slipping and bits of wall tumbling or being dismantled by wild campers, the villa inching inexorably towards the cliff edge, but they were in the fabric of my cove, parts that I visited, inspected, occupied whenever I returned. Yes, I never for a moment imagined that the cottage really was inhabited by wreckers nor the villa by Romans – those were childish designations, throwaway notions of a piece with sailor ghosts and headless horsemen – but as each was described in these pages, its coordinates plotted, its dimensions recorded and its use postulated, that easy familiarity receded into statistical lifelessness.

And as I pored over the particulars – 'a garden, or similar', and a structure that was '[p]robably either a store, or a mason's shed', and another that was 'possibly a building platform', or '[p]erhaps a storage area for slates' – I felt once more that I was not gleaning anywhere near as much information as the wealth of detail appeared to promise. I read that my ledge was 'probably' a point for loading finished slates into boats, which bemused me given the great mass of sloping rock beneath. The wreckers' cottage was 'probably' a pair of two-storey quarrymen's cottages, which might or might not explain the two uninhabited addresses mentioned in the 1851 census. That imagined front door came to mind again, in duplicate this time, opening to nothing but a long tumble and then the ghastly drop into the cove. What gave me pause now was not the building's insanely precarious situation, but the volume of rock that must have been quarried away since it was first constructed, bringing it ever closer to that drop, the edge ever closer to the threshold or thresholds. The cove was surely a different shape when the wreckers' cottage was built. The same presumably goes for the villa: it would have been positioned some way back from the edge with which it has since been quarried and eroded to treacherous contiguity. From the data I gained little insight, other than that 'possible' storage or building platform, into what the villa was used for and when it originated. My money is on a dressing floor, where quarried lumps were split and finished or 'dressed', transformed into roofing slates, leaving behind those strata of slate fragments in and around the foundation – but who knows. The quarry-cove was in a state of perpetual alteration. Loading platforms and stores for machinery or finished slates would have been abandoned, and new ones established as the bedrock – the land – receded. Structures would have come and gone, traces crumbled into air.

So much for facts. Later I would read about the archaeologist, wrestling with this place in the dark early days of 1941: shivering and sneezing, scribbling notes and labels, his fingers almost too cold to grip a pen, let alone write, always hurrying,

always against the clock, the short days and the advancing construction work, the buried things that give every impression of
not wanting to be found. And I would think then that the cove
and its presences, its past presences, could not be known on any
terms other than their own, and I'd wonder who on earth I was
to have thought they should.

I did at least establish from the second report that the cratered mound in which I once hunkered down under the wind
was not, nor had ever been, a tumulus; I had not committed
some unwitting act of desecration after all. The second of the
pair, on the other hand, was indeed once a barrow in which, as
I'd learn elsewhere, the remains of several people were laid to rest
including the young woman with excellent teeth who owned a
bronze pin; from which, some millennia later, they were spirited
away in leaky bags and mislabelled tins. As our archaeologist
raced to excavate the tumuli, the Admiralty was transforming
the common and adjacent farmland into a bombing range.
Two concave lookouts or gun emplacements, one repurposing
the emptied tumulus, both reinforced with slate, would soon
be constructed on the headland – a strategic place if ever there
were one. You would settle down below the scouring wind with
the sea and sky infinitely in your sights. A buzzard might glance
through your crosswires, unaware that the world is at war. A
wheeling, manic-eyed herring gull. There might be a vessel of
concern, or perhaps a plane, or porpoises leaping, carving fluent
shapes through air.

*

The sea is silvery on this late-summer day: argentiferous, as galena is. Galena, a seam of silver-lead so potentially valuable that a Victorian mining company sent men thirty fathoms below sea level here at Tregardock. It turned out to be a short-lived venture – extraction was interrupted by a dispute over royalties with the Duchy of Cornwall, and abandoned within a decade due to poor yield – but it was an ambitious one. That men equipped with hard hats and candles might spend their working hours in sweltering, noxious underground confinement, routinely risking death, tempting fate with every inhalation, every step on a ladder or walking board, every detonation, every blow of hammer on chisel is, as it were, hard to fathom. That they might do so not merely deep in bedrock but deep beneath the shore, a wooden door closed against tidal surges, the sea's echo still audible at the easternmost inland reaches, taxes the imagination. Surely that is somewhere – not a place so much as a medium – beyond the limits of where a person ought to go. What must it have been like?

'Our path was a strange one, as we advanced through the rift'. Scrambling, crawling, climbing, creeping. In 1850, around the time that work began on the new shaft at Tregardock, Wilkie Collins descended into a full-blown submarine tin mine at Botallack, further south, and reported back on a disorienting milieu of pitch dark and flaring flame and 'hot, moist, sickly vapour'. Pits and dead ends and hiatuses traversed by planks and cross beams. Narrow platforms over darkness. 'Lumps of ooze': form in formlessness, or formlessness in form. You may feel a sense of déjà vu as you read these passages: they are written under the influence of Miltonic and Romantic hells, the poetry of darkness visible, and they flex descriptive and melodramatic muscles that would find full range in Collins's fiction, most famously *The Woman in White*. Or perhaps it is those eighteenth-century etchings of imaginary prisons, prisons of the mind, that you saw in a Left Bank print shop on a rainy Saturday – their lightlessness and their spatial non sequiturs haunt you still – or that you are prone to a murky recurring dream from which you can never quite free yourself. Collins nevertheless describes a place that is weirdly and improbably real. How else would you come up with the idea of salt water 'percolating through invisible crannies in the rock': the sea above?

It was not uncommon in the nineteenth century for 'travellers' or tourists to visit working mines; Murray's *Handbook for Travellers in Devon and Cornwall*, first published in 1851, includes advice on planning such a visit. You would be furnished with some mining clothes, a hard hat and candles, and a miner would escort you into the shaft. You would undoubtedly, as Collins did, chip your own souvenir from a seam of ore. The twenty-something novelist, yet to find fame, was backpacking around Cornwall with a friend in an idealistic quest – worthy of Wordsworth, consentient with modern hikers everywhere – for 'untrodden ground'; for wild or 'savage regions' beyond the reach of the railway network, which then terminated in Plymouth. They made their way around the coast from Looe to Boscastle and took in, inter alia, Botallack Mine, the grave of the frozen sailors of Beacon Cove and, hot on the heels of Tennyson, Tintagel. The following year, as that new shaft was deepening at Tregardock, Collins published an account of the pair's West Country adventure. Today *Rambles Beyond Railways* makes for a callow and whimsical read, with social observations that are rather less than edifying in tone – and yet, in places, Collins's prose participates in wonder.

Here he is again in Botallack Mine, in a deep gallery where, as the little party crouches silently, 'a distant, unearthly noise becomes faintly audible':

> *a long, low, mysterious moaning, that never changes, that is felt on the ear as well as heard by it – a sound that might proceed from some incalculable distance, from some far invisible height – a sound unlike anything that is heard on the upper ground, in the free air of heaven – a sound so sublimely mournful and still . . . that we continue instinctively to hold our peace, as if enchanted by it, and think not of communicating to each other the strange awe and astonishment which it has inspired in us both from the very first.*
>
> *At last, the miner speaks again, and tells us that what we hear is the sound of the surf lashing the rocks a hundred and twenty feet above us, and of the waves that are breaking on the beach beyond.*

Maybe it was something like this at Tregardock one-hundred-and-eighty feet below the mermaid's door. But Collins has something more to report from beneath the sea at Botallack. Above the heads of the little group a hole is stopped by a large wooden plug that is keeping out the sea. In stormy conditions, their guide continues, the percolating salt water 'spurts out furiously in thin, continuous streams' and the noise is so 'terrific' – prodigious, terrifying – that the miners down tools, fearing for their lives, and retreat to the surface.

If Collins came to Cornwall looking for untouched nature, for wildness conventionally defined, he found in the industrial site at Botallack something altogether wilder, an outer limit of human intervention in the natural world. That limit is nerve-shreddingly approximate. 'Immense wealth of metal', his miner guide tells him, is contained in this dripping roof, 'but it remains, and will always remain, untouched'. The valuable object of the miners' excavations also constitutes 'their only protection against the sea', and in parts has been worked away to a thickness of three feet. 'No one knows what might be the consequence of another day's labour with the pickaxe on any part of it.' Whether you are a miner or a quarryman, under the sea or underground, or for that matter at a cliff face, these bald facts are a parable in the making.

Yes, today the sea is silvery: argentiferous, as galena is. It is mid-August, mid-afternoon. The fields are colours of ripe grass, gold through tin. In hedgebanks and thickets on the way down from the farm green berries are fully formed and tinted with potential: a faint darkening thrown like shadow across a cluster of green elderberries, a brownish cast on tight green rosehips caught by the sun. Green haws green, or bronzing green, or brightening to orange. Green and red and purple blackberries, ripening with no discernible reference to light. Green sloes growing dusky, as days do.

The gorse and the heather. A huge, heaving silveriness when I came out on the clifftop above Tregardock. *There's the sea! I can see the sea!* I turned and headed for the cove; the northern horizon was shimmering, the church insubstantial and afloat.

I followed a butterfly down into the valley, a pearl-bordered fritillary. It flew just ahead as if showing the way, holding the zigzag course of the path. It paused from time to time on heather or yarrow, and the undersides of the insect's closed wings were like the leaded glass of a Tiffany lamp. As I drew level it fluttered off again, down the path, flying low, and when I was almost at the bridge the butterfly vanished.

The cove is bright, and like the sea the slate is silvery. At first, when I jumped down out of the gulley, out into the light, the cove felt smaller than usual, the enclosing cliffs lower. But now that I am on the far side of the rocky slope, looking up at the sliced cliff face, the upper strata of slates in earth, everything rears in a way that feels chaotic and, despite the silvering light, dark: overwhelming.

I have turned away to investigate a small rock pool. It is almost rectangular, and at each corner is a round hole that must once have held some kind of bolt or rod. To sink this cavity to such regular dimensions would have taken a fair amount of mechanical force. The water is pellucid – it dissolves the light – and the bottom is encrusted with pink paint weed and planted with minuscule sea plants. There is a delicate whitish bush that warms to gold at the tips of its branches, and an olive-green one with a shaggy form, and a dull-red plant with rounded fronds that I took at first for sea anemone. It amazes me that, left to their own devices, these tiny plants have spaced themselves around the pool with ecological and aesthetic precision befitting a careful gardener. There are two grey topshells; several small, greenish-ridged limpets; and one periwinkle. Barnacles have cemented themselves above the water level.

I wish I'd brought a magnifying glass, for the four holes are miniature worlds in themselves. I am on my knees and one hand now, peering as closely as my back and balance will allow, holding my glasses on with the other hand. One hole contains a horizontal stack of tiniest, thinnest slates. There are grain-sized pebbles in the other three holes and, adhering to the sides, minute limpets that I can barely bring into focus. And, now that I have my eye in, I can see that dark specks at the bottom of this bit of captured sea are moving under their own steam and have tentacles, and are in fact juvenile periwinkles barely emerged from their larval state into visibility.

Then I look up at the cliff again, and my head swims and I feel a little sick. It's true that I have been looking very closely; it takes a moment for eyes to adjust, especially when you are on the wrong side of early middle age. But still the way those oblong façades tilt and tower above my head makes the fibres of my being flex and tense with fear. I know that rushing momentary blindness from my secondary school days: the ringing in my ears, the numbing of my jaw, the real danger of being sick. I don't understand my own panic at first. And then I do. It is not just that, when I crane my neck back, the rock looms and lurches as if it is falling on me, though it certainly has that effect. A touch of vertigo is nothing compared to the bodily knowledge that, from the top of this sheer face, you have very nearly fallen to your death.

I need to go back to the cove, I don't know why, I had told Shaun. Then go, said Shaun, but you better be careful. He stayed behind, working.

I took regular breaks on the motorways – I'd promised I would – and drank too much coffee as a consequence. I sang along, no holds barred, with Springsteen and Freddie Mercury. Thoughts occurred and wandered around as they are apt to do in the cogitative space of a long solo journey. That piece of slate with its right-angled nick had – so I believed – changed everything; it had shown me through my fingertips how little I knew about my cove, made it instantly unfamiliar. The cove may have slipped through the methodical net of those environmental and archaeological surveys, but my new-found curiosity was undiminished. It was also very general. What I was looking for, and how I might unearth it, I didn't know. I suppose I was still trying to make up for fifty years of ignorance.

It was easy, of course, to pin everything on a bit of slate. Things between the cove and me had been changing, getting complicated, for quite some time, roughly since my mother's death. Increasingly the cove seemed unpredictable. As of course it must always have been, as coves, interfaces of land and sea, by definition are; it is just that, for the first part of my life, I hadn't felt it to be so. More to the point, there had been times in recent years when I had felt estranged from the cove, or the cove had palpably distanced itself from me. A few strange things had been happening here. Was it me, or was it the cove? Was it possible to tell? I do not think I still believed that hard information alone was the surest way to get the measure of the place. Going back to look for facts was really about going back.

The car sped downhill to the Tamar bridge almost of its own accord. KERNOW: I opened the window and breathed in deeply. Soon I'd be keeping an eye open for that first sighting of Rough Tor.

Late in the afternoon I checked into a bed and breakfast on a farm several miles north of the cove. Maria, my host, welcomed me with tea and an enormous slice of lemon cake. I dispatched a second slice, and wondered what I ought to do next: I'd come to Cornwall on my own and without a plan. In the event, after unpacking, I got back in the car and drove to Tregardock and started walking north. I didn't make it to the cove; dusk was setting in when I reached the common, and the sea had grown pale and mysterious. I turned back. Out in the thickening atmosphere, as I drew more or less level with the tower, a bright speck flashed suddenly and vanished and flashed and vanished and flashed and vanished, the rhythm of the lighthouse at Trevose Head. A few steps on and the light was gone.

I was eating fish and chips in front of the news when Maria tapped at the door. Oh god I'm so sorry – the smell. No no, said Maria, not at all, I just want to ask if you're OK, down here on your own. You seemed – I hope you don't mind me saying this – you seem, well, there's something sad about you. Sad??? I double took. Me? Sad? Here, back in my bit of Cornwall – my happy place, my safe place? Not at all, I said, I was missing my husband very much, he was called Shaun, but no, I couldn't possibly be sad. I'd wanted to come back so very badly and, well, here I was. I moved to perch on the edge of the bed and offered Maria the chair. I was fine – more than OK, in fact. Maria sat down and accepted a chip. I think you are also sad. I can feel it. She told me that her mother had died a few months ago and her father had been gone almost two years, and that they were buried together up at Boscastle, a stone's throw from the sea. That she and Ken had been together since school and were like that (interlacing her fingers), and had three children, a grandchild on the way, but that she sometimes woke up in the small hours and felt lost. I told her about my childhood holidays down here, and how it was still difficult to look at photographs from that time, my parents gone. About my parents' ashes and the cove. How I had not been able to say goodbye to my mother and how, decades on, that disproved the maxim that time is a healer. We talked about things that had happened to her family, and things that had happened to mine. Maria stood up and hugged me good night, the chips long since finished. You need to take care. I will, I said, I promised Shaun, I know the cliffs, the forecast is dry: I'll be absolutely fine. I'm not talking about the cliffs, she said, you should take care.

Maria was right. You can get a long way by denying sadness, but you can't deny it out of existence. *We had joy, we had fun, we had seasons in the sun, / But . . .* there is always a but. Don't be a silly billy, my mother had said, but my distraught eight-year-old self had had a point with her catastrophising bedtime prophecies. It is true that nobody had got cut off or drowned – not yet, at least – and no one had fallen off a cliff, though my mother had come heart-stoppingly close, nor been brained by a tumbling rock. But I'd worried that my mother and father would die, and so it had come to pass. Will everything be alright? I had asked my mother. Some things were, and some things weren't.

I opened the window wide before getting into bed, and slept a sleep deepened by the cool sea wind. I woke early with the sea light, and I felt light. Today I would be going to the cove. Ken served me eggs and sausages sourced from his farmyard. Then I slung my boots and backpack into the car – careful on the cliffs, Ken shouted – and set off on my day. I picked up a mobile signal at the top of the hill and pulled over. Keep in touch, Shaun had texted, let me know where you're going & be sensible on the cliffs. It's not as if I'm a cow, I pinged back with a bovine emoticon. Sorry, I followed up, that was crass. Of course I will xxx.

It had never taken me so long to walk to the cove. I looked

and pottered and fiddled around. The day blustery and brilliant, thyme in bloom at the edge of the cliff; I watched a bumblebee work the mauve flower heads, braced in the wind, holding on. The tiny aromatic leaves glittered as the sea glittered. The thrift was almost over with, and the sea light lent a soft sheen to the spent papery globes. The church a mirage. A lump of rusted metal was embedded in the path. I prised it out with the tip of a walking pole: it was bullet-shaped, some kind of shell I thought, and more or less fitted in my hand. I put it in my backpack with a view to adding it to my bits and pieces from the cove – mermaid's purses and fragments of slate; a bird skull, driftwood, sheep wool, a rusted bolt – that clutter my shelves and window-sills and desk, for it is hard to leave the place empty-handed. Everything shimmered in the wind. I nibbled on a lacy carrot flower, and its herbal taste deepened to earthiness. Something struck me about the clifftop and the high fields where the tower was: 'much green just here, very . . .' Whatever I scribbled is blotted out by a scrap of chamomile foliage that has dried into the page like ink.

I was close to the headland when I wondered whether it was such a good idea after all to carry a bit of old ordnance about with me, especially one that was not merely heavy, but appeared intact; come to think of it, it seemed like a very bad idea. I could hardly put it back in the path for someone else to step on, nor toss it into the scrub where another red cow might come to grief. In the end I clambered around an outcrop close to the edge of the cliff and pushed my find deep into a recess on the seaward side. The sea beneath, churning. I decided not to mention the matter to Shaun.

It was almost high tide down in the cove. I looked at the

paths that criss-crossed the other side of the valley. There were two ways inland, and of course the coast path that I trod now, and the ever-narrowing path to my ledge. And there were others, the old coast path that threaded up around an eroding edge, and quarry tracks, and myriad interconnected paths like veins that led nowhere in particular. I decided to walk each of them in turn because it was high tide and because they were paths. I scrambled up earthy ruts and skidded down others, took the ghost coast path up the valley side and stepped gingerly back down some kind of track that seemed too steep to have been designed for human feet. I walked out to my ledge and back, and then I climbed again to join a grassed-over quarry path. It was straight, and inclined very slightly uphill, and as I walked it seemed – a pleasing impression – to lead me infinitely west. When the sea came back into view, as it did suddenly, I stopped. The ground gave a little as if it consisted of nothing but incomparably springy grass. I shifted my weight back and forth, feeling the lightness beneath my feet, drinking in the light on the sea. Below, on the cormorants' rock, a single dark iridescent bird embraced the west with outstretched wings. *This. The light. The salt-bright light. The ocean. All of it.*

Later, the paths all trodden, I climbed back up the other side of the valley and perched on the outcrop above the wreckers' cottage. A brisk wind blew from the open sea; it stung pleasantly through the sun on my skin. I looked back across the cove, taking in the sheer cliff, the shapes, the angles and the paths. Above one of the sliced façades a path ran beyond the edge of the cliff, grass and thrift underpinned by air: that springiness beneath my feet, the rocks below.

It looked like the breaking edge of a wave.

III

The Tower

I had that dream again, for the first time in a while. The walls of slate are leaning in: the darkness, the glistening. The drizzle and the salt-smoke smell, the thunderous sea, the muffled echo of my mother's voice, the piled waves advancing. I know that there is no way out. I am cold. I cannot move. I am petrified.

The fear must have been there all along, a deep seam like the galena that runs beneath Tregardock. It surfaced at those childhood bedtimes, when deadly edges and inundating tides were ready forms for a protean anxiety, and in the unsupervised roamings of sleep. On the ground, in person as it were, the cliffs and the coves and above all my cove were places of freedom and happiness, of safety from the worries and terrifying peers of my youthful everyday. In adulthood sad things, awful things, strange things had attached themselves to the cove – but not until I looked across the valley and saw that scrap of overhanging thrift and turf did I know real fear there. Even then the fear was retrospective – for precisely when I should have been scared witless, when I was very close indeed to falling to my death, I was drinking in the light and salt, the weightlessness beneath my feet, watching the cormorant watching the sea, absolutely content.

That dream resurfaced more than once in the following days. And in my waking hours, moreover, I saw my mother – really saw her – on the day that she too very nearly fell from the cliff. I did not recognise it at the time, though I was behind her and saw the things that, in adulthood, I would replay with horror. My parents had made so little of it when it happened, or rather almost happened – protecting us, and themselves no doubt, keeping the holiday soaring and innocent. I am older now than my mother was then. I watch her stride ahead of me on the bright path down to Beacon Cove, Treacle at her heels. Her every movement bespeaks happiness and I see now as, aged ten, I sensed but could not conceptualise, that she feels free, in the moment, not just my mother but herself. She is hurrying, flying along – she cannot wait to cross the narrow ledge and clamber down to make the day's first footprints in the sand – and at the corner she stops short and the abruptness makes her seem to sway. I hold my breath and my heart beats faster as I examine those details from forty-five years ago. Now, as my mother turns around, I can see that she is shaken, shaking. I see how close our lives came, in that moment, to changing forever. And the rest of the day that my mother nearly died is lost to me.

Quarries are dangerous places; so are cliffs. Where does that leave quarried cliffs, I wonder? I'm looking with new eyes at a familiar photograph. It was taken by my father in that privileged time, more precious than we were aware, before Beacon Cove was cut off from us. My mother, my siblings and I are sitting on various rocks at the foot of the cliff. We're tucking into sandwiches amongst a clutter of boots and socks and Thermoses, bananas, paperbacks. My mother is wearing her anorak and I am wearing my mother's sweater, which is very much too big for me, and my own anorak arranged around my waist like a skirt. My bare toes are scrunched up, working the sand. Spread out in the sun on a rock of their own are a green sweater, a pair of jeans and sundry smalls. It's the day on which, arriving safely in the cove, I tore off my boots and socks, rolled up my jeans and ran to meet the sea. The sand was wet, and as the waves withdrew they left temporary copies of themselves in foam. I waded out, bobbing over shallow waves, sand draining thrillingly from under my feet, and out of nowhere a forceful little wave knocked me flat. Behind us in the photograph is the great angular gouge through which we have descended. I can see slate rising vertically from one side of that narrow ledge, falling vertically from the other, and I see now why I used to sing so loudly – *I can see clearly now the rain has gone* – as I hurried across – *All of the bad feelings have disappeared* . . . There is the corner where, though you cannot see it from this viewpoint, a hole is widening; then the path runs along and up the cliff and out of the frame. And I see that this recess must, like the recesses in my cove, have been quarried at some point in the past, and that the elements have only done one part of the erosive work.

Ought we ever to have been climbing down to Beacon Cove? I will never know. I am glad we did. In Beacon Cove it was always going to be a bright, bright, bright, bright sunshiny day.

*

The tower bugged me. I was ambivalent about its mysterious acquisition of UPVC windows. My mother and I had talked, of course, about putting in windows and looking out of them, gin and tonics in hand, but that dream belonged to us alone. Over the years, furthermore, the abandoned structure had settled into the landscape – at least, into my landscape – and now it had a suburban aspect that seemed out of keeping with its surroundings. Even so, I wanted to look out of those new windows and see what I could see, no matter that the tower rose no higher than the roof ridge of a two-storey house. A tower was a tower.

As a zealous latecomer to maps, I had tracked down most if not all of the sheets pertaining to the cove and its neighbourhood. The tower was not to be found on any of them. Not even, especially not, the Ordnance Surveys; military structures, for obvious reasons, are not marked on the versions destined for public use. One day I unfolded the 1:25 000 and studied the shapes of the fields at Treligga, and tried to work out which one contained the tower, for on the ground the boundaries are an indistinct complexity of posts and wire. And I saw the dotted green line of a footpath running parallel to the coast, linking the hamlets that lay just inland beyond the clifftop fields. It would lead you from Tregardock to Treligga and Trebarwith and, should you turn off at Trollope's letterbox, to the cove. Why had we never walked this way to the cove? Why would you take an inland route when you can be beside the sea? Now, though, I was curious.

On a billowy March day in the year after my teetering near miss, Shaun and I set off past the former pigsty, down the track and then, instead of heading on towards the sea, we struck out on the new path: *Tregardock Treligga Trebarwith Treknow.* Fields stretched away to the ocean, speckled with livestock. The tower in green distance. We came to Treligga and lost our bearings: the hamlet was labyrinthine, of an intricacy that seemed incommensurate with the modest area. Slate walls spun off every which way. Forking lanes returned us by various routes to an ivy-shrouded Victorian letterbox, another of Trollope's, probably. The ivy had put on new growth of a shade almost too tender for evergreen. The place seemed full of converted chapels: we counted at least two, and the hamlet was very small indeed.

A farm track led us north again. Hedgebanks and green verges, earthy herbal smells of spring. Fields and ocean glimpsed through gateways. An old sign: NO ADMITTANCE. Ewes called and lambs responded. A cluster of tumbledown slate buildings. One roof lay almost perfectly collapsed on the ground as though the barn or cottage had slowly deflated, the largest slates still graduating from the eaves to the smallest where the ridge had been. I lifted one from the outermost edge of the heap. It was weighty for such a thin thing, and all the greys in the world were contained in its textures and mottlings. Mica glinted, and rust veins ran through the underside. Half of the upper side, exposed to the elements, had darkened with centuries of weathering and was crusty with black algae. The other half bore a single hole that was clogged with rust from an iron peg. Histories must be layered within the slate like sedimentary rock. Stories of mud and seismic events. Of men who extracted and cut or 'made' the slate in one of the surrounding quarries. Of those who built the barn or cottage and pegged these slates to roofing battens in an overlapping weatherproof configuration. Of people who lived or tended livestock under this roof; of hard livings. Of Atlantic weather and dereliction. Of who knows what next.

The undulating surface of the slate was like a piece of sea.

Another gateway: look! Rumps Point, Puffin Island. The tower maintained its air of remoteness but was very much closer than I'd seen it before, and partially framed by sea. The colour of the sky grew from distant washiness to a rich intensity overhead, and clouds were suspended in low inverted ridges like weather made for a theatre set. The edge of the land ran left to right and dipped into a blue-filled V: the cove.

The track continued through a locked gate – PRIVATE KEEP OUT – to farm buildings, and our path angled off to run alongside a hedgebank of roughly laid slate. Blackthorn dense along the top, foxgloves leafing up in crevices. The edge of the field was waterlogged to put it mildly; we splashed through grass in water, then through mud under water. Springs rise here and descend by one route or another to the sea, and if you should stop now and let your mind fall still you will begin to hear what is not so much a sound as the audibility of a watery place.

A chimney took shape amongst the thorns, and another one. That struck me as strange. At the end of the field two widely spaced slabs led us up and over an intersecting hedgebank. Pausing at the top to unhook the barbs of a bramble from my sleeve, I noticed a bit of railing amongst the lacerating shrubbery. It was galvanised, more in keeping with a school playground than a Cornish hedge – though unlikelier items have found their way into the incidental infrastructure of farms. I held the thorns back with a walking pole. A metal staircase led down the other side of the hedgebank, and though what lay beyond was private property the stairs demanded, having been revealed, that someone descend them, and so I did.

Foxgloves grew from this side of the hedgebank too, and bracken, campion. A primrose in bloom. It was sheltered at the foot, warm though the season was early, and utterly quiet. A long low breeze-block building blocked the Atlantic wind. Each end terminated in a perpendicular section, and the two corners lent an idea of enclosure to the grassy space. There were not two but three chimneys, and grid window frames that in some parts had corroded to nothing and in others still held glass. Ivy grew in and out of the apertures. I picked my way through brambles and bits of debris. Shattered glazing and lumps of asbestos crunched beneath my feet. The first window gave into a small room the walls of which had faded or deepened to a kind of salmon yellow. An empty light socket dangled from the ceiling, and on the back wall hung a lovely vintage radiator. Through the next window I could see a Bakelite light switch and a fir-green door. Emboldened, I stepped around the end of the building. A heap of rusted metal and brambles. Another one of slate and brambles. Bathtubs, sundry junk, water tanks. Concrete piles and broken asbestos sheets were stacked neatly against the trunk of a spreading hawthorn tree.

Then I lost my nerve, and hurried back to the steps. It wasn't the best idea to be tramping around amongst broken asbestos, but I was rather more concerned about the possible consequences of trespassing; if you have ever been a child on the wrong side of an irate farmer, not to mention of the farmer's hedge, that special blend of terror and guilt will entrench itself in your lifelong habits. I remember hurrying up the lane in Sussex, out of breath with the hill and the sobbing. What's happened? asked my mother. I can't tell you – it's awful. Tell me. I can't. I did something. It's awful. What did you do? TELL ME. It can't be as bad as that. I – I climbed the gate into Mr Donaldson's field. I was going to see if the blackberries were ready. And then – Mr Donaldson came, and—

From the distance of the coast path these low buildings at the furthermost end of Treligga had every appearance of agricultural purpose. I knew that the paradoxical topography – the chaotic, cratered common to the north, the strangely level expanse to the south – had to do with the remodelling of an ancient landscape in time of war. But I'd assumed that the installation had long since been dismantled or repurposed, give or take an intractable bunker or tower and rusted shells that the land heaves up every now and then; I'd happened on another one recently. And here, now, were the buildings themselves, abandoned and dilapidated but intact, with radiators and bathtubs that intimated everyday lives. They had been here all along, all these years that I had walked the coast path: masquerading as a farm, hiding in plain view.

Shaun and I walked on over the fields and dropped down to cross a stream amongst feathery, deadly hemlock. It was, I saw later on the map, tracing the rising springs and contour lines, the very head of the valley that curved and carved down to the cove.

Then we joined a lane that wound into Trebarwith, another slaty place. The farm, the wall, Trollope's letterbox. We turned left and leaned for a while on a gate at the top of a track. Beyond the fields was a sea-filled V so regular and crisp, so close to equilateral, that someone might have cut it out of the land with some kind of precision tool. As soon as we set off down the track the V stretched and lost its shape. The stony hedgebanks and streaming springs, a complex smell of green and muddiness and cold stone and herbivorous dung. Red cattle on flashes of grass amongst the hawthorn branches.

Many a Trebarwith quarryman must have walked this track with his brew can and packed lunch. At a bifurcation he might have turned into the holloway for Trebarwith Strand and the big cliff quarries, or continued on the track as it wound around and then headed, straight as a Roman road, across the northern valley side to the cove. We left the track sooner, at a muddy bend, and descended over fields and through bracken and scrub to join the stream on a lumpy cattle path. The ground grew marshy at an intersection with a short, lateral valley that carved its way down from the direction of the tower: what I used to think of as the stream is in fact one or other of two streams, or their last-minute amalgamation just before the gulley. All those springs obeying gravity. The banks of the main stream were miniature cliffs of loose earth flecked with slate. The valley sides steepened and the ground grew chaotic, heaved up into lumps and crags. The sheltered spot with the mounds of thyme. Did you smell that? What? Cigar smoke. No. Oh.

The erstwhile V swung back into view, now an amorphous dip. It held the sea right there, at eye level. The cove head-on. The water had a strange tint and appeared to move steadily, incessantly towards us. My stomach pitched with an old sensation that was not quite vertigo, and before I knew it I was in the mood world of that petrified dream.

When Norden made his survey of Cornwall around the early 1600s, he found the cliffs to be 'verie high, steepe, and harde', like 'a defensive wall againste the continuall furious assaultes of the prevayling *Ocean* on all sides'. Were they 'of a more earthy or tender substance', like the shingle on which the drowned

Sussex town of Old Winchelsea was built, they 'coulde not have so long prevented *Corn-walls* utter obsorpation'. He somewhat overstates the case, but modernity did not invent coastal erosion. 'Obsorpation', as the word is printed in my edition, is an aberrant spelling of 'obsorption', an old word for absorbing or swallowing up. Maybe the typesetter made a mistake or someone had poetry in their soul, for there is eloquence in this accidental hybrid of 'absorption' and 'obliteration', 'inundation', that you will not find in the dictionary. Obsorpation is the sea's instinct. Both in meaning and on the tongue, the word articulates awe: a sense of sheer magnitude, of impersonal power held in check – so far, just – by the hardest edges of the land and the moon's influence. Obsorpation: that's it, exactly. The thing that filled a dreaming child with dread and turned her momentarily to stone.

And then I hurried on ahead, down through the dark-walled gulley, the stepping, the slithering, the gravelly crunch, out into the light, the listening, and there was wonder in the cove.

The tide is still going out. The slate slope is wet, and left-behind sea has stilled in the shallow depression. To all appearances the pool is set in pale-pink rock – a quiet pink, the colour of fading thrift. In fact the slate is encrusted with layers of paint weed, a coralline alga which, being rich in calcium carbonate, is as hard as rock. *Lithophyllum incrustans*, encrusting stone leaf: the botanical name translates with the spare eloquence of a haiku line. Several indentations, roughly oval like the New-Agey ring marks I have noticed elsewhere, are scored into the pink stoniness; some have been scraped or worn to holes of gleaming slate, their pink edges flaking as old paint does. The pool is dotted with limpets, constellations of slightly wonky conical shells – and when you look down on them their radiating ridges do bring lopsided stars to mind. A flat periwinkle is interfering with one of them – its motion is purposeful, its antennae busy – and now and then some animate speck or other flits through the water and vanishes. Otherwise this pink pool appears to be the limpets' domain. Who knows what a cup of its water would yield to a microscope – but so far as the naked eye is concerned there are no other molluscs or cnidarians, crustaceans, echinoderms, and certainly no other seaweeds, not a minute branching hint thereof.

The limpet is moving deliberately across the pool. Hold on, you hear your reader say: how can something with a mere smattering of neurones be capable of conscious intent? Yet the limpet is, in some unintelligible way, moving deliberately. The shell appears to be gliding, hovering of its own accord, for the hairy tentacles that extend from the ridges barely skim the rock, and although you know that a creature inside is moving on a single muscular foot you cannot but read these protuberances as myriad feet because they are visible and because, if you yourself were some kind of maker charged with giving the limpet feet, this is where you would put them. Your eyes also tell you that the mollusc is moving in slow motion. They are wrong; it is moving in limpet time.

This extraordinary creature, a common limpet, has reached a cluster of those ovate holes. It pauses momentarily at the largest one, and as it begins to turn you realise that the space and the shell have similar dimensions. Both taper at one end and are far from symmetrical: the ridges of the shell are formed at irregular intervals, and jagged indentations are arranged unevenly around the edge of the hole. Slowly and, yes, deliberately, the shell effects a series of tiny manoeuvres. It eases its edges into place, closing every last infinitesimal gap. Without the aid of parking sensors nor, for that matter, a brain, the limpet has parked perfectly in its so-called home scar, every ridge fitted to its corresponding indentation, tentacles retracted, stuck like a limpet. You wonder whether you really saw what you have just seen; had you chanced upon this pool a minute later you'd have been none the wiser. You wonder whether anything surpasses the marvel of a limpet coming home to roost.

Yet somehow, somewhere, in some capacity, this mollusc has a memory. Its homing instinct is astoundingly strong: the limpet possesses, as you have just witnessed, an exact sense, right down to the last indentation, of where it belongs in the world. It goes off foraging, especially at high tide or at night, and often returns home by a different route. It scrapes up food by means of a toothed tongue or radula that might give many a carpenter's file a run for its money. Though these radula teeth are strong enough to deal with calciferous weed – they are made of the strongest biological material known to man – limpets graze by preference on green vegetation. Paint weeds thrive in the absence of green; the pink interior of this limpet's pool is a sign of overgrazing by its inhabitants.

Limpets might be brainless, yet you cannot think about their instinct for home without using words that pertain to consciousness. How can it be that this creature has some kind of memory? Wherein does memory consist? How do you know where you belong?

In southern Britain limpets spawn in rough autumn seas, the rougher the better. They spawn any number of analogies too. They roam and graze like herbivorous mammals; they come home to roost like seagulls at nightfall, bats at first light. They park themselves like cars – like boats – like the UFO in *Close Encounters of the Third Kind* – like all and none of these. The figurative tables are turned when people talk about tenacity – yet the substance that makes a limpet stick like, well, a limpet is the self-same mucus that enables them to move, to travel away from home: its state can be reversed at will (so to speak) from adhesive to lubricant, and so on. Nor is the limpet unlike certain highly evolved mammals in that its longevity is inversely proportionate to the convenience of its food supply. Those that live amongst plentiful weed grow fast and have an average life span of two to three years; those with homes on bare rock, obliged to travel for their forage, grow more slowly than their sedentary over-nourished peers and may reach the ripe old age of sixteen.

One thing is unambiguous about these mindless, mind-bending molluscs: their capacity for violent self-defence. Even a starfish's hydraulic power and insidious solvent biochemistry are no match for a mature limpet. Threatened by that finger-like prospecting touch, the limpet will rear and crash its shell – the edges are hard, and applied with force – down onto the offending limb, and again, until the predatory echinoderm backs off. How the non-centralised nervous system of the starfish registers pain is anyone's guess, but you bet that hurts.

The pool fallen absolutely still, the scored shapes in the pink-painted rock, my limpet stuck fast in one of them, parked in its place. So keenly had my right-angled piece of slate alerted me to the shaping influence of humans that I took those ring-like marks in the rocks to be artificial too. But as it turned out, they were not prehistoric cupmarks like those in the tumulus up on the headland, and definitely not the work of some more recent pagan: the ways of my wild man-made cove were more mysterious than that. Limpets had ground the grooves into rock by twisting their shells, creating thereby a tight seal against water loss and predators. In each home scar, each bespoke foundation for the mollusc and its portable housing, a limpet will stick like nothing so much as itself.

The frenzy of research prompted by my slaty enlightenment was fruitful in a way that proved richly contrary to my purpose. It laid bare my presumption that the cove could be plotted, anatomised, charted; historically and archaeologically explained and thereby, somehow, *properly* known – grasped, owned through information. I had lived through that season of estrangement, when the cove grew strange to me and I perhaps to it. I'd had to find my way back – a way back in myself, I suppose, for I never stopped returning on the ground. Then, after picking up that piece of manifestly hand-worked slate, I'd begun to enquire into quarrying and geology, and sixth-century Celtic missionaries, and the building of the North Cornwall Railway, and wandered off into historical monographs on pilchard fishing and wrecking. It was an education if not in the world of my cove, then in its universe – but little stuck to the cove itself, and my greatest lesson from it all was an obvious fact to which I'd been blind. The cove was still my cove, as it was when I was young, before the grief and the making strange, but it was also not my cove. It was not anyone's. The cove was the cove: it was its own place.

The other thing that happened when I picked up that L-shaped slate was this: all at once, in and around the cove, I saw human interventions everywhere. The straight edges and angular gouges; the approximate geometry of the inverted footholds down through the gulley; the mysterious ovoid carvings on sea-smoothed rocks. The limpet had corrected me on the latter count.

And then I acquired a second piece of slate; it weighs about the same as the first. The upper surface is the same colour, if brighter, the underside rusty, and its edges form a thick near-rhomboid that almost fits in my hand. It is of a piece with the phantom blocks that, removed for one reason or another, left those tilting non-steps behind. One afternoon, climbing out of the cove as the tide crashed into it, we saw that a section of the gulley wall had cracked and the slate loosened. Shaun jumped across the stream and rummaged carefully. I quarried this for you, he said upon his return landing.

The jointed structure of slate is such that it often fractures naturally into rhomboid lumps. They may be sizeable and serviceable blocks, or pieces too small for any purpose other than holding in your hand. Their interior angles may stretch and narrow beyond the regular, but broadly speaking they behave very much like quadrilaterals. Once you have come to see the cove as a quarry, as a place of hacked and cut, finished and unfinished slates, you may confuse these angles and parallel edges, the rough geometry of geological structure, with the work of human hands. But there are straight edges and straight edges, or at least straightish ones: those sawn with tools and those formed by natural joints. The cove has angles and it has angles.

*

I ought to be working, but too much is going on outside my window in Northamptonshire. The sycamores at the bottom of the garden are shedding their last leaves, the rooftops and meadows beyond inching back into view. The sun is low though it is almost noon, and the air stirring. A ragged elder, still green in leaf, is briefly and breathtakingly luminous; shadows come and go across the grass. The rookery has all but disbanded for the year. I miss the birds' chaos, their gregariousness, though they mob the red kites and their guano wreaks havoc with the paintwork of the car.

Given my inborn longing for the sea, it seems more than a little ironic that we have come to rest about as far from the coast as it is possible to be on mainland Britain. Shaun and I arrived here by accident after years of moving homes and countries. I am happy in this Midland place two-hundred-and-ninety miles from the cove. I love the big skies, the woods, our friends. And the sheep. The other day I watched a hare move across a ploughed field, and its form was charged with grace. Often our nights are traversed by owl calls; the red kites cruise and swoop through our days. I am watching one move amongst the treetops now, a streamlined form with bifurcated tail, wholly self-possessed in the absence of the rooks. And yet I long for my bit of Cornish coast. I long for the cove. A recent scare or two notwithstanding, I feel different when I am within its sphere of influence: a little more at one with the world, a little more myself.

I am poring over a six-inch Ordnance Survey map, published in 1907, of the area surrounding the cove. I often visit the cove on maps these days. I can scarcely believe that I did not so much as look at one until I fell in love with a man who loves maps – but then, as I have said before, I thought I knew the way.

Since then Shaun and I have walked tracts of mainland Britain together, and I would no sooner set off on a hike without a 1:25 000 than I would without my walking boots and poles, or water, or Tunnock's caramel wafers. But when I look at the cove in its successive Ordnance Survey settings – I have tracked down most of them, starting with the 1883 first edition of the six-inch series – what I see is a representation, neither map nor picture, vivid as a photograph but differently so, of a complexion in time and over time. The gradient lines and the graphics signalling quarries, marshy ground, streams, the church – and, on the old twenty-five-inch sheets, just about every rising spring, every pore and follicle of the land.

Back on my six-inch sheet, a tattered photocopy, I notice that some things have changed in the twenty-odd years since the first edition. The North Cornwall Railway has appeared in the bottom right-hand corner, snaking around the tip of the Delabole quarry. Up on the common some kind of structure has disappeared from the cliff edge. Working quarries are scattered over both editions of the map but are concentrated along the cliffs above Trebarwith Strand and on the sanding road past Penpethy, where Hardy sought his greenish slates; a couple have fallen into disuse between the two editions.

Methodism, the faith of the Cornish labouring classes, is ubiquitous. There are nonconformist chapels, mostly Wesleyan, in Trewarmett and that morsel of village at Delabole; another in Trebarwith, two in Treligga. You will find plenty more should you step from this sheet up towards Tintagel or down through Delabole to the quarry settlements and Trewalder and St Teath.

Over at the cove I recognise most of the tracks, but the map shows only one or two structures predicting the ruins on the ground today. The twenty-five-inch versions tell the same story in greater detail: the spot, for example, that I once designated a turning point for Roman chariots is labelled a quarry in 1883 and unmarked in 1907. Stores, sheds, dressing floors might have been and gone by the time the survey was refreshed for the second edition; coastal quarrying, as we know, was a transient business. But the tiny shape of the wreckers' cottage is there. And here's a thing: the two streams do not appear to converge as they do today, but rather to follow separate courses linked by some kind of straight channel. The shorter, lateral stream turns sharp left into the main valley and then heads for the gulley, the cove. The main stream courses down through the valley and continues straight along the path to my ledge. I cannot tell whether its flow is definitively diverted through the channel at this point, but one thing seems clear: the tunnel did not conduct sheep to their doom after all, at least not by design. As recently as 1883, in fact, it is clearly marked as a footbridge.

By 1907 the active human work on the shape and shapes of the cove must be substantially done, the usable slate quarried away, scullocks left to the elements – though some years possibly remain of hacking and shovelling those naturally fracturing lumps, maybe even of drilling and blasting. The contours of the cove at this moment in time are lost with their last living memory; our Trebarwith quarryman's daughter is already twenty-two years old.

A notification pings on my phone, but I do not attend to it: I am down at Treligga now, in the bottom left-hand corner of the six-inch map. This part of the map intrigues me too, for what I have only ever known as a flattish breadth is, in 1907, a complex of ancient field shapes together with an extra southerly section of the common. A track runs amongst the fields, connecting the clustered hamlet with the common grazing. I run my eyes around the shapes of the fields, seeing their outlines into dimensions of slate and soil, gorse and thorns: Cornish hedges.

I look at my phone. The text message is from our friend Pete, who lives and farms in Treligga. He's sent me a photograph taken from the top of a field that rises behind the hamlet. I know the field. I can see its shape on the map right now; in fact, I know the very spot from which the photo was taken. The field slopes down to meet the houses. Beyond is that familiar expanse, greener than when I last saw it. There is the tower, a rectangular speck. The edge of the land and a band of Peloponnesian blue, a V-shaped nick – the cove – and then a band of sky-blue sky. I text Pete back: Not again! I was just looking at your place on a map.

This kind of thing has become quite normal. Back in the summer, on a train, I fired off a text: Sorry haven't been in touch. How are you all? Calves doing well? Now you're at it, came the response, I was just texting you. A version of the afore-described view, with sheep and foxgloves and dulling grass, followed moments later. Then there was the time when Shaun asked me if I had heard from Pete lately. The phone rang in the bottom of my bag, but I was driving. It's silly, I said later, returning Pete's call, we were talking about you when you rang. Yes, he said, well, you know how it is. That cove of yours . . .

I first met Pete a few months after we'd found our way to Treligga. It was late summer, the cove was calling me, Maria had a vacancy, Shaun said go. On the first morning, on my way to the cove, I made a detour around The Mountain to watch the long waves at Tregardock, to be mesmerised by their sound and their successiveness. I stood on a low elevation above the beach, and time stilled. I do not recall whether the tide was coming in or going out. There is a perpetual rumble in the air here, a rolling and dragging, the ocean's quantity draining back below the surface. A periodic crack, a wave breaking like rock splitting, and always an undertone the like of which I have not heard anywhere else. You could almost believe that the special resonance has something to do with the mine shaft under the shore, just as sounds are transformed and amplified as they travel through the plumbing in apartment blocks. It is loud, yet somehow sounds more distant than it is, distant in time as well as in space. Maybe you are listening to the sea's absolute distance from the human scale. The sea is indifferent. Unless you happen to be a poet, it tells you nothing – you cannot tell someone something if you are not aware of them – but in that audible remoteness you hear of your own significance in the scheme of things.

I don't know how to put it all into words, I told my mother back then, when I was nine. Now I know that it won't be put into words, though I cannot stop trying as I've done for decades on and off, jotting things in notebooks. Words are human things and the sea will not be contained by them. It is, as Whitman wrote, a continual miracle. You reach out, writing, for what you cannot grasp.

It is also easy to indulge in elevated sentiments like these from the assumed safety of terra firma. You must respect the sea, as fishermen and lifeboat volunteers do. Unlike writers and holidaymakers, fishermen have no choice but to involve themselves with its brute unfathomable ways; lifeboat volunteers choose to do so in the service of others. But the little boy who died in a rip current down there on the dark beach was only jumping waves at the edge of the sea. He would be fifty-five now, as I am. Sometimes that Tregardock rumble is the sound of an unspecific dread.

Not, of course, that you should make assumptions about the safety of dry land. I thought of my mother all those years ago, stopping dead on the edge of a vanished path, and I thought back to a more recent morning when I myself nearly walked off the cliff above the cove. I wondered what had made me stop when I did, why I hadn't taken just one more springy, deadly step. I wondered how on earth, as it were, that overhanging bit of green had held up under my rocking weight. And as I watched the heaving and breaking, listened to the gravelly drag, I found myself in no mood to walk on north along the cliffs and, coming over the headland, be confronted by the grassed path opposite, its abrupt end.

Instead I headed back inland and took the footpath to Treligga. The thorns and tamarisk were shapes of waves blown from the sea. The verges flanking the track to the airfield were high with late summer. Tansy and angelica; hogweed gone to seed. The nettles had peaked, and a single acanthus had escaped from a garden and was flourishing. The foxgloves blasted and knobbly. Someone was working a sheepdog nearby. Cheerful commands carried on the still air and were interspersed with a veering, hysterical *mehhhhhh*.

I continued as far as the padlocked gate and leaned on it, contemplating the derelict buildings. The place fascinated me. I was desperate to take another look, but the padlock and the PRI-VATE sign were unambiguous. Then again, there was nobody around. I climbed the gate and took a few steps, and then I lost my nerve and climbed the gate again. I was small when that Sussex farmer yelled at me, and all I could recall afterwards was a fleshy angry mouth and the knowledge that, in hopping over a gate to look for blackberries, I had done something very bad indeed.

I walked back along the track, following the sounds of the sheep, and found a farmer penning them in a corner of a field. Two dogs crouched and patrolled in attitudes of busyness, being important though their work was done. One sashayed over as I crossed the field, his pink tongue lolling, pleased with himself. The farmer had an air of kindliness. I was so sorry to disturb him, I said, he must get sick of straying hikers. My name was Beth, by the way. His was Pete. It was just that, well, I was curious about the old airbase, I explained as I scratched behind the collie's ears, in fact I'd been slightly obsessed with the tower since I was a kid, and I was just, um, wondering whether I might take a quick look around. It was his land, wasn't it? No, those fields belonged to David. David was at a livestock fair in Okehampton and wouldn't be back (*aha*, I thought) until evening. I jotted the name of David's farm in my notebook; I'd look up the postcode and write to him later. The sheep were clamouring. I thanked Pete very much; I should let him get on. Oh, he was in no hurry; in fact, he had an old postcard that might interest me. What about the sheep? They had shade, they'd be fine. The dogs scrambled to attention, and Pete headed over to the house.

The browned monochrome photograph was probably taken in the early 1900s, around the time of those revised Ordnance Survey maps, from a high point in a sloping field. It leads the eye down amongst grazing cattle and over Treligga, over a commanding white chapel, to a quintessential patchwork of old fields defined by Cornish hedges. The land undulates like a heaving sea, and the dark swathe of the common extends some way into the frame. The old fields are too numerous to count – I'll do that another day, when I sit down with the maps – and they stretch from the hamlet to the edge of the common and out to the edge of the cliff. Had the photograph been taken with a fractionally wider-angled lens it would include the cove. There is no sign of a tower. In the grainy brown and white I can see that the sun is in the south-west, picking out some fields brilliantly while others are clouded over. Inside the photograph the day is green and blue, a day of fast clouds and lively light, as this one is.

Pete suggested that we take a walk. The dogs led the way up behind the farmhouse. There, Pete pointed out, was a reservoir that once supplied the airbase with spring water. Over there was the old farm quarry; the slate stone that it yielded was not the best quality, but perfectly adequate for walling things like barns and all these hedgebanks. It all came back to slate in this place, he said, slate was there, everywhere, just beneath the surface of everything. It was even in the walls of those military buildings, for the breeze block was substantially composed – a marvellous example of wartime vernacular – of crushed slate spoil from the Delabole quarry.

I wondered aloud what it must be like to actually live here. I'd been coming to this part of the coast for a good fifty years, and I loved it more than anywhere else in the world. But I could come and go when I wanted to; what was it like to live and farm in this place? Well . . . it went without saying that you couldn't make much of a living from farming alone any more. Most people had another job or two, maybe a second business. Many were diversifying into tourism, holiday lets, that sort of thing.

The price of wool had plummeted – people wore synthetic fleeces these days, didn't they? – but the price of feed had not. And obviously you couldn't control the weather. In a good year you might lay in more than enough hay and silage, but a cold dry spring followed by a hot dry summer could cost you a fortune in winter feed. What about Brexit, the EU subsidies? Hmm. Who knew how that was going to go. And the – um – tourists, and the second-homers? Hmm. The region was chock-a-block for several months a year – sometimes you couldn't get the tractor out for all the parked cars – and it was just, well, a shame to have so few neighbours out of season. That must be hard to take, I ventured, all those empty homes and local people priced out of their own property market. And then of course, Pete said with an indefinite gesture, there was this. *The light,* I thought. *The ocean. All of it.*

Anyway, what was I doing out here on my own? I should be careful on the cliffs; and in any case wasn't it a bit lonely? I was rather more cautious that I used to be, I said, maybe it was my age, and admittedly I'd spooked myself recently, had a bit of a near miss. We talked about the cove, the unpredictability of the way down, the hidden corner with the wavy sand, the fishy-smelling cave. The problem with those corners, said Pete, was the getting back again; you thought you were on top of the tide times, but you never quite knew.

He hadn't heard about the boy who drowned at Tregardock; that was a while before he moved here. He could see how something like that could happen. You always – *always* – checked the tide times before you went down, but once in a while the sea would behave weirdly. It might not go out very far at all before it started coming in again, or it would spread about in ways that you couldn't quite read. The further reaches of the beach would be there tomorrow, but you only had one life didn't you? A Swiss climber once said the same thing to me apropos of mountains.

At the top of the field we turned and followed the hedgebank until Pete said, about here, and stopped. The postcard view was before us, and it was not. I ran my eyes between the landscape and the photograph. Hedges and trees had grown up around the buildings, obscuring the white chapel, and there was an additional house here, a missing building there, but Treligga was still Treligga. As I looked up from the postcard, though, what I saw beyond the hamlet that day was not so much a familiar landscape as one that had been erased. Almost erased: one or two of the vanished hedgebanks had left faint lines that were smudged with scrub, and where the southern half of the common had been the grass was browner, rougher than the adjacent green fields. Once you got your eye in, Pete explained, you could see how the head of the lateral valley, just beyond the tower, had been filled in and built up in a massive earth-moving operation. The modern wire boundaries of the fields were all but invisible, the tower out there in their midst. I would so love to go to the tower, I said, to climb up inside and look out from the windows; I'd been wanting to do that for as long as I could recall. I supposed the tower belonged to David too? It certainly did, and – for Pete read my mind – in David's absence the tower was very definitely out of bounds.

*

The sea seems strange today and the air is restless. When I came along the cliff path gusts snatched now and then, and in between all was preternaturally still. Down in the cove four cormorants, alert forms, looked west from their rock. I followed their gaze to an unspecific dullness at the horizon. A named Atlantic storm is due to make landfall at the end of the week – I saw the mass swirling and jerking across the weather radar at breakfast – but yesterday, when we stood and looked out from the top of the field, Pete said you must always keep an eye on the horizon. Today is only Thursday, a bright August day but for that far-off shadowiness. The stream is diminished, and though the slate walls drip and ooze in sunless parts the going is easy enough: I stepped and jumped down through the gulley in no time at all.

But for my yellow booklet of tide tables – I checked the times before I left – you would not believe that it is almost low tide. The ocean is up there in front of me, in the cutting at the mouth of the cove. The waves are streaked with unearthly turquoise, lit, or so it seems to me, from within. They heave, break, and the sound does not push and recede but pushes and pushes as though the sea were out of patience, pressed for time. There is no question of clambering around the slope today. That warm wind setting in, waves bumping edgily against the rocks. I promised Shaun I'd be sensible and in any case, down here in the cove, I am feeling rather – I don't know what. Alone? Listened to? Certainly small. That said, I have my feet on the ground: I cannot fall from here.

Seagulls flap and scream momentarily above my head. The screams travel on around the cove, louder and harsher, primitive, and in their wake sounds a long diminuendo wail. I have not heard many birds today: I couldn't put my finger on it earlier when I walked down amongst the hedgebanks, the thorns, and crossed the common where linnets busy themselves in gorse.

There is something more than thrilling about a rough sea colliding with the edges of the land; the rougher and rockier the better, I've always felt from a just-about safe distance. It absorbs you wholly, viscerally, and the drama and the thunderousness correlate with a stilling at your core. You cannot explain this, only know it. But a slow-heaving sea like the sea today is another thing altogether. It shifts and drags with a latent power that fascinates and unsettles you: you feel it in your stomach rather as you feel dread. And at the horizon a shadow is darkening, spreading like a stain.

The tone of the sea is darkening too, its rhythms lurching. It works at the rocks with uneasy restraint. I am growing uneasy too, but I cannot leave. The piled waves push and break on the spot. The tide has not obviously receded, let alone advanced, since I have been standing here; I think about what Pete said, how once in a while, in some places, the sea will make a mockery of our *Tide Times* booklets. I am standing at the back of the cove on my usual rock. The stream is implicit in the shingle, a watery shadow of itself. I want to move closer to the waves, but something is holding me back. The wind is steady, warm and odd. I am a little out of sorts, as the day is. My head is aching – it often does when the barometer drops – and I feel alone; I am alone. Shaun is hundreds of miles away in London, and I miss him. Maybe I am not supposed to be in the cove today. I think that perhaps I should leave right now and go up over the headland to Trebarwith Strand where all the people are, and buy an ice cream and watch the holidays unfolding on the beach.

A gull shrieks and scuffles somewhere above, though I'll only notice this with hindsight. Rushing air skims the backs of my legs, and a sick thud throbs in my head. A very heavy object has fallen behind me, cracking against the edge of my rock, splatting in the sodden shingle. I turn around, look down. And freeze.

The lump of slate is roughly the size of an A4 ring binder filled to capacity though its angles are squashed and stretched. There are smudges of iron oxide in the greenish sheen, and the block has fractured and splintered to reveal a rust-bright interior. I am lucky to be alive. I look up at the cliff and realise, though my eyes have passed over it innumerable times, that the loose upper strata really are very loose indeed, and that the earth is no retaining medium for the chunks of slate that tilt and protrude from it. The gull is still fussing on a tiny ledge. It looks pristine, as herring gulls do for all of their filthy eating habits and malodorous breath: the head and neck white as fair-weather cumulus, the grey back smooth amongst the textured slate. I look up into an impassive primrose-yellow eye. Seagulls are remarkably sensitive to the human gaze. A herring gull with designs on your chips or ice cream will stick around, choosing its moment, if you are looking away or at least not directly at the bird. It may well touch down on your head and swipe the cone, as once happened to a man who stopped to chat with us in Lyme Regis; we felt faintly guilty for distracting his attention. If, on the other hand, you look the gull in the eye, stare it out, it may very possibly retreat. It is tempting for a person to take this for self-consciousness. I've no idea whether I have established eye contact with the gull above my head: I know it sees me but the eye is unreadable. The thing has no idea of the consequences of its shifting and flapping about – and even if it did, I decide, feeling rising like the waves, even were it possible for a bird to feel remorse, this one would not.

You bastard. You nearly killed me.

The sea has taken on an eerie patina. Mackerel clouds are seeping landwards, filtering the sun. The waves are making a sound like gravel.

I'm hurrying now, across the shingle, the attenuated stream. Up through the gulley, smashing my feet into planes of slate, their adverse tilt like nightmare steps, forcing my way up through the air as if through downward volumes of water. Across the stream and straight up the valley side, the coarse grass and the slipping earth, rabbit droppings, shards of slate. At the top, out of breath, I pick up a signal and a text from Shaun: Everything OK? What are you up to? Fine, I reply, this and that, sausages for breakfast, weird weather, off to Treb Strd for ice cream. How are you? Missing you.

Now, in the warm wind, I am shivering.

Later I will think of the nine lives that cats are said to have. It is just a saying, of course, a way of speaking about the heart-stopping intrepidity of felines, their devil-may-care agility. That said, a close call on a motorway may leave you viscerally unsure whether you are still alive: maybe you are not alive, but having a dream or memory of being so, or perhaps another life has indeed been granted you, picking up seamlessly where the previous one left off. Either way you move through the next while with a kind of heightened attentiveness: you are acutely conscious of being alive, but in what capacity you are not quite sure. You feel a little, I don't know . . . ghostly perhaps, like the listeners or the Traveller in their disjunctive realms. You scrutinise your conversations and interactions for signs of some such change, but so far as you can tell from the behaviour of others you seem to be you and you seem to be here. Cautiously, at first, you get on with your life, whichever one that may be; you are starting to feel that you have used up your fair share down in the cove. You cannot stop going back, though: the place may have nearly claimed your life but it is still, somehow, your safe place. To that extent alone the cove has made a revenant of you.

*

Three women are sitting on grass with their backs against a breeze-block wall. They are sharing a tray with white china cups, an enamelled coffee pot, and a plate heaped with angular biscuits like slates. Two of the women wear simple dresses, the other a dark regulation shirt, and wind is mussing their rolled hairdos. All three are laughing and gesturing with thumbs-ups and victory-Vs. They cast crisp shadows: the day is sunny. To one side are a large radio device and an unoccupied wicker chair.

Three different women are sitting or kneeling amongst ripe grasses. One holds a small dog. The women lean slightly into the frame; the dog stares straight into the lens in the uncanny penetrating way of dogs. Behind them rises a steep bank covered with scrub. It looks like a spot for a picnic, though one woman is attired in a nurse's uniform and another in one of those regulation shirts. I wonder whether, nearby, a metal staircase with a galvanised handrail ascends the Cornish hedge.

A young woman poses like a screen goddess. She is chic in slacks and a fitted blouse; her lipstick is impeccable, and her pinned hair is loosening and lovely in the wind. Something about her expression reminds me of my mother in a photo from the early fifties, though the likeness dissolves in a flash. The woman is leaning, hand on hip, on the post of a barbed-wire fence. Wisps of snagged fleece catch the light, and the background is an indistinct expanse in which, if you peer into the monochrome, you can make out three or four sheep. Beyond, not that you'd know it from the photograph, are sea and sky, and if you followed the edge of the land rightwards you would soon find yourself at the cove.

In the next photograph – I love this one – a woman bundled up in a military-issue asymmetric duffle coat moves in on the camera, brandishing a snowball. The snowball is small and looks hard, eminently fit for purpose. Snow covers the ground and the corrugated roof of a breeze-block building in the background. And it is snowing in the photograph: flakes splatter the foreground like paint, falling too fast for the shutter speed. The woman's hair blows straight back from her face and everything about her speaks exuberance. Her right hand is raised to lob the snowball any second now.

I'm standing in a corner of a windowless hut in the old RAF base at Davidstow, now the Cornwall at War Museum, and though it is stifling I have goosebumps on my arms. A succession of 1940s photographs is passing over the screen of an old monitor to upbeat British Pathé music. Most were taken at Treligga, though in one or two I recognise the coast of Port Quin or Port Gaverne, further south. The installation cannot be paused or fast-forwarded, so I see each black-and-white image for a fixed number of seconds and then I must wait for the loop to end and replay all over again. It takes time, but I have no specific plans for the rest of the day.

But for the odd uniform and the breeze block, these images might have been unearthed from a box of family photographs. People of my grandparents' and parents' generations (the Treligga women are somewhere in between) taking tea or picnicking, leaning on fences, sitting on gates, holding cats or dogs or babies, larking about in that unspontaneous way necessitated by the cost of film and the rigmaroles of manual exposure. In that box are young or younger faces of people from a time before I knew them, and faces of strangers: family friends and friends of friends and distant relatives whom I have never met, or do not remember meeting, and whose names I now will never know. The Treligga images overlap in visceral ways with photographs taken a decade later when my mother was around the age of these young women. She sits on the South Downs and raises a cup to her lips. She perches on a fence, laughing, her hair tousled by the wind, and again on a field gate with my aunt, and stands with her arms full of an old spaniel called Paddy, who stares imperiously at the camera. She even has an oversized forces duffle coat with those tell-tale one-sided toggles; it's a cast-off from a cousin, and she is wearing it as she walks towards the camera in a snow-white lane flanked by inky snow-lined trees.

Ghosts are stirring, tears stinging, as these oddly familiar images of unfamiliar women come around on the video loop in the corner of the airless hut. Something else about the photographs moves me too, in a way that I cannot pinpoint. Women drinking coffee, sitting in the sun, posing, having a laugh, making snowballs in wartime. It has to do with the quotidian, an impression of everyday intimacy, of cheerful domesticity – for the camera, at any rate – in settings made slightly strange by bits of uniform and unhomely breeze block, a Bedford truck, the quadrant tower (it *did* have a staircase, after all).

Now ten or twelve women stand around a piano. They are singing, and their attitudes are slightly contrived; you don't get this kind of visual harmony, everyone looking to the pianist, by snapping your subjects unawares. This time all the women are wearing dark shirts and sporting immaculate victory rolls. Daylight streams in through the windows behind them. The metal window frames are familiar though I have only peered through them from the opposite direction. I recognise the distinctive panelling of the door and know, from those glimpses through broken panes, that in the world of colour the woodwork is a rich fir green. On the piano is a large jug of foxgloves; it brings a touch of the front room to the uniformed scene. It must be summer. Beyond the windows, outside the photograph, foxgloves flourish in a hedgebank. Their purplish spires were over with on an August day when, the landowner safely away at a livestock fair in Okehampton, I nipped back down the metal stairs to look in through those windows again, and the tower, now explicitly out of bounds, seemed further off than ever.

Most of the women in these photographs wear some permutation of the Women's Royal Naval Service or WREN uniform: dark or white shirts and dark ties; dark skirts or stylish matelot trousers; dark sailor sweaters. Some sport tricorn hats and officers' stripes, others duffle coats, one that nurse's uniform. They pose against the walls of crushed Delabole slate in varying degrees of formality; the tricorned officers, when they do appear, smile stiffly. Three women in sweaters and bell bottoms perch on an asbestos roof. The uniformed occupants of a blurred dormitory are snapped in apparent haste. Four women sit at a long table set for many more. A woman takes something out of a Rayburn while her companion rubs flour and fat in a mixing bowl. Another sits alone at a refectory table, writing; her form is out of focus, ghostly in the cavernous room. An ungainly figure encased in something not unlike a space suit is led calmly by sou'westered colleagues through low ridges of smoke; the suit, I learn, is also made of asbestos, and the firewoman inside is a farmer's daughter called Rhona. A similar lack of urgency suffuses photographs of first aid drills enacted against backdrops of Cornish hedges. Out on the clifftop, in visible gales, duffle-coated women are occupied with lamps and flares, telescopic Aldis sights and viewing frames; wrestling with a distended windsock; training binoculars on sky.

Now, at last, they are in the tower. The brick walls are unfinished, but the windowsills are faced with bullnose quarry tiles like the ones in my Sussex bedroom when I was small; I love that detail. In one photograph some kind of chart is spread out on a table next to a window; a woman leans over it, plotting a line with a ruler and drawing pen. In the next, three women are gathered around a different window. One is looking out through binoculars, another through a telescope, and the third is speaking on a telephone or pretending to; there is more than a hint of contrivance in this one. I wonder, when the camera has been put away, how far these women can see, whether they have ever spotted a porpoise or a peregrine. Maybe even a chough, black as its relative the rook but trimmed with scarlet legs and bill: there is still time, a good thirty years, before the bird's extinction from this place. I know it is wartime, but I envy the women in this captured moment: I would give almost anything to sit at that window with the swivel-mounted telescope.

Towards the end of 1939 plans were drawn up at the Admiralty for the compulsory purchase of Treligga Common and adjacent farmland, about 240 acres in all, and the construction of a bombing and gunnery range for air-to-ground and air-to-sea target practice. The site, known as HMS *Vulture II*, would be a satellite of the Fleet Air Arm's training base, HMS *Vulture*, over at St Merryn. Its chief purpose was the training of pilots in the Arm, the branch of the Navy that operated aircraft from carriers at sea. This involved rather more than setting out a few targets on the clifftops. The angle of each dive and the accuracy of each attack would have to be measured with quadrant instruments and recorded. Targets must be not only set out, but constantly repaired. A reinforced concrete hut was required to protect personnel and equipment from shelling, and a control tower for the coordination of each exercise: incoming pilots might have to be diverted because of some hitch on the ground, someone still hurrying over to the bunker, a calibration problem, a farm horse grazing in front of a target. Emergency landing strips were required in case a plane should suffer engine failure or ricochet damage. The site was too small to accommodate more than wheels-up or belly landings, but in the course of the following year field systems would be grubbed up and massive volumes of earth moved around, a tumulus accidentally sliced through, the head of the valley filled in, the ground levelled to create three grassed runways. Fire and crash tenders were needed too, of course, and medical support, telephone lines, signalling equipment, accommodation blocks. Not to mention, as a preliminary 'Schedule of Building and Structural Requirements' sets out, a flagstaff, noticeboards, and heating for the officers' control hut. The document to which the schedule is appended takes it as read that the base would be staffed by men; it was a reasonable assumption in 1939.

In the event, the only man posted to HMS *Vulture II* is a Royal Marine driver who billets in the hamlet. The base itself is manned, so to speak, entirely by women and has been for the past two or three years since canvas-hooded Bedford trucks delivered the first Wrens; that was in the autumn of 1941, some months after the archaeologist had departed with his tins and bags of human remains. The Marine driver claims to be the brother of a well-known movie heart-throb; he bites his nails but is, all things considered and in the absence of competition, reasonably fanciable. There are about thirty women in the ship's company, as it is properly called; HMS *Vulture II* might be built on slate, but it is a naval outfit through and through. With the exception of the officers, most are in their late teens or early twenties; one of them, later in life, will write up her recollections of this time.

Upon notification from St Merryn that an exercise is due to begin, some Wrens head for the control tower to man telephones and Aldis sights, others to the bunker and quadrant equipment; others help Rhona into her asbestos suit and stand by with fire engine and ambulance. The bearings of each bomb and rocket are calculated by triangulation, and the readings passed back to St Merryn. For all of their infernal noise the exercises are routine affairs.

There are rotas for cleaning and boiler stoking, tending the kitchen garden, fetching milk from the farm. Trips to the cinema at Delabole, and to Wadebridge for shopping. There are negotiations with geese. The women carry out rescue and first aid drills. They play hockey on the airfield – sheep graze there too – and tennis on a court adjoining the vegetable garden. Rhona tests her asbestos suit by sitting on the galley fire. Someone makes banana from boiled parsnip and banana flavouring; I think that almost makes sense from a textural point of view. Someone else has a copy of a steamy novella by Somerset Maugham, from which she reads choice passages to her dormitory mates. In summer the women cut foxgloves for the jug on the piano. One winter there is an unprecedented fall of snow; HMS *Vulture II* is snowed in for a short while and, as we have already gathered, there are snowball fights. The whited-out landscape, one Wren will recall, has a 'curious and dramatic effect' on the sea, lending it the appearance of 'watered soot'. There is an exquisite precision to this image – but I would love to see the snow scene for myself much as, for all those years, I longed to see a rainbow over the headland.

Down below, old tracks have been repurposed. One of them leads from Treligga Common via the shorter lateral valley. Out on the headland the emptied-out tumulus has been revetted with slate and a second, matching crater constructed nearby. Maybe Home Guard volunteers hunker down inside them, prone, training binoculars and gun sights on the westward sea. It is as strategic a spot as I can imagine, whether you are a Bronze Age community, or a twentieth-century militia on the lookout for enemy invasion, or a nine-year-old getting the measure of immensity. There are telegraph wires in the valley too and, in the middle of one field, a telephone. Amongst the farm tracks and quarry tracks, the ruins and the earthworks, the blackthorn, the gorse, decommissioned tanks are positioned to train pilots in machine-gun attack from low-flying aircraft, a practice known as strafing. The planes fly in close over the cove, and automatic gunfire reverberates apocalyptically around the walls of listening slate. Up in the valley amidst it all, the gunfire and the engine noise, the tilting swooping flying machines, red cattle graze on unperturbed.

*

I have an image of the cove that is more vivid than any photograph. On that day of eerie light, the storm below the horizon,
it burned itself into my mind's eye in the seconds before I turned
to get the hell out, the crashing slate and the gull's deadly innocence, the sudden unreality of being alive. I sometimes look
at this panorama in the small hours. It returns with a forensic
clarity unmatched by anything I have seen on the spot, looking
around in real time. The world blurs at moments when you feel
your existence to be under threat; mine does anyway, for panic is
blind – yet later you may revisit in hyper-vivid detail where you
were in that wave of sightlessness. This happened to me a good
many times at school. It happened again in the seconds when
I realised that I would never take proper leave of my mother –
and again, in the moment that a falling lump of rock narrowly
missed my head.

This image is not accompanied by any sound, nor seaweed
smell, any sensation of sun nor wind; it is just a detailed visual
sweep around the edges of the cove. The land's end, its shades of
slate, grey through brown to inkiness. The lower part of the cliff
looks solid enough. Above the level of my head the slate grows
blocky then foliated. The layers tilt inwards, the cliff sagging as
though it has wearied of its own weight. The rock has fractured
here and there. The uppermost parts of the cliff consist of loose
soil interleaved with chunks of slate. A huge heap of slate and
earth conceals my ledge. Then there is a crumbling edge: the
path. As the cliff wraps around behind me pale earth mounds
and bulges again, the outermost edge of the villa. Bits of slate
are sticking out, and in a small recess a herring gull is shifting

about. I do not like this bird. Thrift and grass spill over the cliff, but my eye homes in on the unretentive soil and the jutting slate: a picture of precariousness infilled with my knowledge of what is just behind this scene. My ledge – it always seems, these days, to be strewn with new slates – and the ever-narrowing path that leads to it: one foot in front of the other, lean away, don't look down. The edge of my villa foundation at one with the eroded cliff. I run my inner eye around these edges, over and again.

Another chunk of slate looks poised to drop: it is positively hanging from the cliff. Surely it is going to fall, any minute now. Two of its edges have been crisply cut by natural cleavage or men with tools. It shines green-grey in the stormy sun and its veins are rust. It makes my heart thump.

How could my safe place be so dangerous? Or rather, how could somewhere so dangerous be my safe place? I suppose it depends on what you mean by safe. Until a recent scrape or two, physical safety barely occurred to me when I was there in the cove, in the moment; it was, of course, another story with that dream from childhood, and at those times when you ought to be asleep but are not – times, as every insomniac knows, when the danger of falling is at its height. Being safe was cantering along road verges and wandering off into woods alone for hours on end; it was hurrying along narrow slaty edges and jumping across weed-slippery rocks to get to the sea's immensity. Being safe was being me.

*

I have been watching the rooks and the shadows of the trees, fiddling with the stones on my desk. Again my fingers have settled on the inner angle of the L-shaped slate. I treasure this bit of quarry waste. Compressed within its edges and surfaces is, if not the shape of the cove, then the story of its shaping. The blasting or shovelling-away of the cliff, the accidental rebuilding with heaps of spoil from its quarried substance; the work of cold, salt, wind and waves. This slate is, in every sense, the very fabric of the place.

I'm turning the piece of slate over in my hands, considering it. The scored hairlines, undetectable by touch: the slate-maker would have used a notched stick to mark up the slab before trimming it with a special knife. The foliated layers or laminae: they might be separated further with chisel and bettle, as the quarryman's mallet was called, split to the thickness of a roofing slate. It was tough, delicate, highly skilled work, for slate is contradictory stuff, hard and resilient yet easily shattered by the business of its extraction and cutting, its 'making' into finished slates. At least seventy-five per cent of slate extracted at the cove would, for reasons of quality or collateral damage, have been unmarketable. Some of these 'deads' would have found use as roofing and walling for farm buildings and labourers' cottages in surrounding hamlets, not to mention the sheds, crib huts, bridges, retaining walls of the quarry itself. Maybe the roof of that collapsed barn at Treligga originated here. I should give Pete a call, it occurs to me, we haven't spoken for a while, they must be lambing by now. My phone pings.

What happened to the rest of the spoil, the bulk of what was quarried here? Much was dumped back over the cliffs, furnishing the ever-expanding cove with raw material for its rocks and shingle, feeding the sea. Much was heaped up or left where it was, new ground formed incidentally, loosely, layering up with earth and thrift, slipping and crumbling and falling with the elements and time. One piece has found its way to my desk: I'm smelling it now, inhaling deeply. The mineral scent is as old as the hills.

The text is from Pete. That cove of mine.

I wonder what the cove was like when Tennyson walked these cliffs in the middle of the nineteenth century. A busy landscape undoubtedly: machinery and donkey carts, tracks and smoke, all kinds of structures. The odd boat. Maybe men are hacking and shovelling down there or even, when the tide is out, hammering wooden wedges into cracks below the high water mark; the wood will expand with successive tides and split the rock apart. Maybe – just maybe – one or two men are standing, if that is an appropriate verb, at the northern cliff face. Hitting and twisting an iron jumper over and over and over again, drilling in excruciating slow motion. Shaping the cove.

The cove is like a sketch. Not a careful one like the future Mrs Hardy's representation of Trebarwith Strand, but a sketch in the truest sense of that word: a rough, unfinished outline. A rapid elaboration of pencil marks on an off-white sheet of wove paper approximately five-and-a-half by eight-and-a-half inches in size. It is executed by someone who is used to taking visual notes – who sees into what he sees before him and knows without really thinking about it what he wants to take away. The paper is slightly wrinkled from moisture and three corners are foxed, stained with brownish marks. The sheet has, after all, been around for more than two hundred years, not all of them in the humidity-controlled vaults of Tate Britain. This sort of thing might also happen if the sheaf of paper in question has been sketched on in sea mist or mizzle; tucked into a pocket and carried around the salty cliffs of North Cornwall.

In mid-1811, nearly forty years before Tennyson's first trip to Tintagel, Turner embarked on a sketching tour of Devon and Cornwall. Always on the move in search of landscapes and human landscapes, he had accepted a lucrative commission for a series of 'Picturesque Views' showcasing the coast of southern England; that the Napoleonic Wars had put paid to travel on the Continent made this an especially opportune time to be focusing on domestic topography. He arrived at Tintagel in late summer.

In the background of this sketch faint pencil lines conjure a headland. The lines strengthen in the middle ground to form an inclining mass of rock. They multiply in our direction, confidently loose, building up planes and dimensions into a chaotic cliff that fills half of the foreground and almost half of the sheet. A rocky shore grows out of an implied space, a harbour or a cove perhaps, between this cliff and the headland behind. A winch or pulley – a poppet head – overhangs the clifftop, dangling an enormous block of rock. Next to it is a similar structure, without the pulley mechanism, from which a chain or rope hangs down the rockface. A vague cluster of marks at its end may be something mechanical, or perhaps a stick man: those two-ton blocks of slate, once loosened, did not secure themselves with chains for winching to the top. At the foot of the cliff three hasty shadings signify something, possibly caves. Huge lumps of rock clutter the shore: rocks, and ideas of rocks and, closer to the cliff, angular blocks. At what point in the sea's relentless work does a hacked or detonated block of slate become a rock? What makes a rock a rock?

As for the tide, who knows. The rocks and blocks, or what you will, and caves are exposed but one or two wavy lines suggest, well, waves. The sketch might be titled *Tintagel: The Haven, with Stone-Lifting Gear*, yet the sum of the pencil lines that bring the scene into being, suggesting rather than illustrating, is more than a specific view. I look at these lines – watch them, I want to say, Turner's hand moving over the paper energetically, back and forth – and what I see is an in-between place of land and sea and human graft: being shaped and taking shape. A cove, the cove, perpetually coming into being.

*

Around midsummer in the year following my eventful solo trip, Shaun and I had the good fortune to stay in Trebarwith. Our accommodation was converted from the original farmhouse, and as we ate our porridge on the first morning I imagined Trollope clattering into the yard to question the farmer about his household's epistolary habits. I'd write more postcards than usual that week because I could step across the farmyard and post them in my favourite letterbox. Children would receive individual mailings instead of the usual family one, and one or two cards would describe in detail the box into which they were going to be posted.

In the lanes and tracks it was the season of pink: of foxgloves, campion, thyme and thrift, herb robert and cut-leaved cranesbills; orchids and rose-red valerian. We hiked for miles along the cliffs. In between, at all kinds of hours, I scrambled up and down and around the valley, trod the cove's edges carefully, and sat looking out to the western horizon with the cormorants.

The common was enamelled with colours befitting the margin of a medieval manuscript. Thyme and chamomile, eyebright and sheepsbit, the tiny ground roses and short-stemmed daisies, burning yellow cat's ears, hawkbits, hawksbeards. I found an adder's sloughed skin up there too.

We walked six or seven valleys in the direction of Rumps Point, and back again with one eye on the sailing clifftop church. We walked to Tintagel for pasties, and Shaun bought me a windmill. Paying for a newspaper in the Spar, the child in me seized upon a bar of Fry's Turkish Delight. But the packaging was all wrong, the rosy foil envelope superseded by crimped plastic in a ghastly shade of sugar pink. There would be no joy in unwrapping this thing and so I put it back. The windmill whirred its colours from the side pocket of my rucksack all the way back along the cliffs. At night we opened the bedroom window, and salt air flooded up the valley into our sleep.

One afternoon we walked down the valley with our host Steve, who farms the gleaming Red Ruby cattle. Steve pointed out how the cropping of turf and scrub by his animals enabled other species to thrive; had we seen the incredible flowers up on the common that week? The conversation moved on to excrement: how the dung of grazing livestock provides, as that of animals kept indoors on engineered diets does not, food and shelter for dung beetles and other invertebrates – a delicate ecosystem also compromised by excessive worming. What is so special about dung beetles? Where to start? They break down cow pats and drag the nutrients into the soil. They are a dietary staple of the horseshoe bats that roost in the cave just over the headland. The chough, a species so iconically Cornish that King

Arthur is said to have turned into one at the moment of his death, also feeds on dung beetles, or used to before it became extinct in these parts. Hope that choughs might one day haunt the cove again rests in no small measure on this iridescent creature that is literally at home in excrement.

We inspected spotted and pyramidal orchids. Milkwort in three colourways: purple, pink and white. Thyme-covered tussocks housing colonies of red ants that might – just maybe, eventually – summon back large blue butterflies. The large blue became extinct in Britain in 1979, but Steve thinks it disappeared from this valley three or four years earlier, around the time of the great drought. Nineteen seventy-six: my year of angst. I remember the endless overheated summer, the parched ground and insufficient air; turning eight on a burning day. The hosepipe ban. A new class in September, growing older without knowing how to. The arrival, one Sunday evening in November, of dread: *We had joy, we had fun, we had seasons in the sun, / But . . .*

It was as if the large blue's vanishing flutter from the cove wreaked havoc with my inner weather all those hundreds of miles away. Stranger things happen, some might say, for if chaos theorists are to be believed, a butterfly may cause a tornado in Texas by flapping its wings in Brazil.

The existence of the large blue butterfly depends on conjunctions of such bizarre and ingenious exactitude that you cannot help thinking it must have been destined for endangerment; in fact, it seems a marvel that the species ever got off the ground. *Phengaris arion* lays its eggs on the flower buds of wild thyme. The window of opportunity is narrow, for the eggs must hatch when the buds begin to open. Throughout the next stage of development the larva or caterpillar feeds on thyme flowers; it will eat a sibling too, should it find itself in competition for a flower head. Next it drops to the ground in the evolutionary hope of being adopted by red ants. To this end it secretes a sweet substance that red ants find irresistible (this puts me in mind of Greek thyme honey, an acquired and addictive taste), and contorts its body in imitation of an ant larva. Worker ants pick up the tempting impostor and transport it into the brood chamber of their thyme-covered nest. All other things being equal the caterpillar will feed on ant larvae for the next ten months before pupating and tunnelling up to emerge as a blue butterfly. Those honey-like secretions, and the creature's capacity to mimic the sounds of a queen ant, maximise the chances of continued hospitality – but all kinds of things can go wrong inside the nest. With a sparse population of ant larvae, or the introduction of large blue rivals, the caterpillar will starve. In the presence of a queen ant the workers may turn on their parasitic guest. Furthermore, several species of red ant will pick up a large blue larva. But only one species, *Myrmica sabuleti*, seems predisposed to accommodate and even care for the treacherous caterpillar; the other species are rather more likely, having lugged it home, to recognise the presence of an alien and dispatch it accordingly. Such evolutionary specificity is brilliant when circumstances align, but the life cycle of this ruthless, vulnerable butterfly has been a game of chance at the best of times. It has little bandwidth for adaptation to intensive farming methods, nor to the unknown quantity of climate change.

For the needs of red ants are precisely calibrated too, each species adapted to subtly different temperature conditions determined by sunlight and the length of the grass. *Myrmica sabuleti* thrives in southerly aspects and closely cropped turf – like this thyme-heaped place tucked into the earthwork where I have settled so often at high tide, first with my parents and then with Shaun, drawn by the special cosiness that accommodates you even when the weather is cool. So sheltered is it that all you can hear is the stream on its way to the sea, the high tide silenced though it is coming and going and breaking close at hand. Whether we saw a large blue butterfly here back in the seventies is just one of many things that it is now too late to ask.

It was yet another paradigm shift to meet someone who not just lived as close to the cove as anyone could live, but who actually owned the land. I didn't know how I felt about that – and who knew how Steve and Marion might feel about the arrival on their doorstep of a stranger with emotional claims to their property. As we walked on towards the cove we talked about the way down through the gulley, how your feet had to find their own way by footholds that were nothing, Steve agreed, of the kind. I'd been doing it since I could remember – my parents carted children and clobber down here all the time – but these days I did catch myself wondering whether it might not be a little, well, dangerous? Shaun certainly thought so. Steve agreed. It was tricky to say the least, and once you were down you had to keep an eye on the tide: that could be tricky, too. People who didn't live around here, holidaymakers, hikers, no disrespect to us, often didn't understand what they were dealing with. You had to be careful. Marion had said she didn't think she would ever go down into the cove again. What, ever? No, never. Really? Really.

Oh and, I said tentatively, I'd been meaning to ask about the ghosts. Anyone could post stuff on the internet, but the cove had also got itself mentioned in a Penguin directory of haunted places. No, Steve said firmly, the place was very definitely not haunted. Later he told us about Uncle Jim, from whom he and Marion had inherited the farm. How Jim's forebears had taken the place over in 1851 (the year of Trollope's visit) and how the family had carried on farming, and the cattle grazing, through the requisitioning and the mayhem of the wartime bombing exercises. Uncle Jim had been gone for years, but Steve still smelled his tobacco smoke around the place from time to time. I took it that this was too normal an occurrence to be filed under ghostly activity.

I woke before dawn the following day and made a Thermos of coffee, and set off down the hawthorn track to see how day would break in the cove. A dog rose bloomed new and dewy in the paling light. The cove was dark and the sea as good as black, working powerfully. As I came out onto the ledge a smell of seaweed greeted me, and evanesced. *Hello cove.* It was cold. The coffee warmed my hands in the metal cup and I thought, for all of its Thermos taint, that coffee had never tasted quite so good. Water rose in banks amongst the rocks, bumping and returning in tangential waves. The sucking little vortices, the slantwise currents like swimming snakes. Waves heaved over the slate slope and drained away to nothing; it was as if someone – a mermaid say, or a misguided miner – had pulled a giant wooden plug from the ocean floor. The waves moved in again and broke, and drained again, and broke and drained, until you could believe that every cell of your body was governed by the rhythms of the sea.

I did not see when sunlight first struck the waves: it wasn't there and then it was, cast from behind the mound of spoil that enclosed me from the valley. Two slates lay side by side at my feet, right-angled triangles the pigmentations of which mirrored one another. They were not here after sunset yesterday, when we sat with a bottle of wine while the sea lightened and the evening settled into opacity. A long time ago someone had started to cut this slate to a roofing specification. It had broken and been added to the spoil heap, and had slid with the elements and time, and last night, falling, split into two triangular slices. They were heavy enough: I was glad we'd left when we did with our empty bottle.

It was still dark enough on the ledge, but sun lit up a corner of the ruined cottage. I'd asked Steve yesterday about the wreckers' cottage. The wreckers' cottage? I gestured up to the crumbled walls, the stomach-churning drop from where, to my mind at least, the front door used to be. Ah, the madman's house. The madman's house? That's what the quarrymen used to call it; they said that only a madman would live in a place like that. Why did you call it the wreckers' cottage? Because only a wrecker would live in a place like that. What did Steve think the building had been? One archaeological report had it down as a winch house. Another identified it as a pair of two-storey semi-detached cottages. A local woman whom we met on the cliff path said it had been a farmhouse. The building had two fireplaces, Steve said, because it was a crib hut. Quarrymen needed somewhere to warm themselves and dry off a bit, and eat their packed lunch or 'crib'. You could say that again. The cold, the unmediated gales and rain, the legion kinds of Atlantic damp. You yourself have been soaked to the skin and chilled to the bone here, at your leisure; now imagine labouring, absolutely exposed, for shifts defined by daylight and the tides. You cannot. A slate-stone shelter, a fug of smoke and wet clothes and body odour, twin fires burning against the odds of working conditions whereof we don't know the half. An idea at least of safety and warmth, and there was hot water for brewing tea.

The wreckers' cottage might have been detached or semi-detached, two storeys or otherwise. Perhaps it was one or both of the addresses recorded in the census of 1851. Either a farmer lived there, or he did not. Ditto a madman, or at least someone mad enough to make their home on that edge. Maybe the edge was not there when the structure was built. Maybe it was a winch house after all. Or a crib hut, a cottage, an abandoned cottage repurposed as a crib hut. Some kind of cottage, Pete has said simply. And beyond that it doesn't matter, for the little building on the brink will always be the wreckers' cottage.

Sunlight had reached the first fireplace. Shaun would be up, making breakfast I hoped, but still I couldn't tear myself from the heaving sea. The power. I sat for a while, shivering, and then something made me look up to the sky. It was pale, promising blue. A bird hovered above my head, its musculature working, vibrating in stasis. I saw the black face and a flash of barred plumage, and before I had stretched my neck quite back the peregrine was gone. It was time to head out into the valley, the bright bright bright bright sunshiny day. I fitted the two slates back together. This broken wild magical place, this place where things perpetually slip.

*

Ten thousand years and more, sea,
You have gobbled your fill,
Swallowing stone and slate!

Thus Charles Causley, conversing poetically with the ocean at Cornwall's northernmost edge. The sea doesn't miss a beat: '*I am hungry still.*'

The inundating, obsorpating sea. Its innocence is terrible: it does what it does. Fishermen putting out to sea from this coast may still, by tradition, greet the waves or say 'hello' to salient rocks, showing respect to immensity, to overwhelming power. That power is overwhelming in the most literal, watery sense (*whelm* is an old word for 'submerge'). At times they listen for the ghost cries of drowned fishermen. Some may be sure that there are cries to be heard. Others, listening, do not really expect to hear anything: they listen for the ghost cries because they are mindful of what the sea can do. There are ghosts and there are ghosts.

September, and in our Northamptonshire garden the Japanese anemones are blooming their hearts out. I grew them from cuttings: they are descendants of my parents' plants that flowered through the first weeks of my life in Sussex. Shaun and I have come to Port Isaac for three nights; a last-minute vacancy was going for a song in a National Trust cottage. It's midweek, the school year has begun, and Cornwall is settling down. You stand a chance of decent weather in September, a month attached to summer, no matter that each of Tennyson's summer trips to Tintagel was a washout. Nor that, in the prodigious storms of 16 August 2004, millions of gallons of water with nowhere else to go flooded down through converging valleys into the harbour village of Boscastle. The footage played and replayed on the news: trees and cars and parts of buildings washing seaward, piling up, people airlifted from familiar roofs and upper-storey windows. Prince Charles and John Prescott visited when the waters had subsided. Over time the devastated village was restored with cutting-edge flood defences and a new, exquisitely arching bridge.

Everything was blue and golden, dreamy, when we arrived in Port Isaac yesterday afternoon. We went straight down to the harbour and picked our way across the top of the beach. I wandered off to inspect a rock pool and found a snakelocks anemone blooming like a marvellous flower. Its tentacles were the colour of jade and tipped with purple like amethyst. Later we drank pints on the little pub terrace, a spot my father loved, and later still we sat amongst lobster pots on the harbour wall and ate fish and chips with copious quantities of ketchup.

The pressure dropped overnight like a dead weight. In the morning the sky hung grey on grey, sagging with moisture and cut through with light. We picked up pasties for our lunch and drove to Tregardock and walked down the track, and turned north up the valley in the direction of the cove. The Mountain's landward flank was reddish-brown: the bracken had turned early and the stems were collapsing into shapes of wreckage, or broken wings.

The church came and went as we walked along the cliff path. A small wind was coming and going too, and fragments of a deep colour broke through the sea's reflective sheen. The sky solidifying. When the tower came into view it was wrapped in obscurity. The atmosphere gaining weight, the sea dulling by the second. My head was feeling leaden too, with the barometric pressure or the grey, or both. A few heavy raindrops fell, testing the air, and then it began to pour. As we crossed the common and came down the valley I noticed only the rain on my face and the sky's darkening, the slate and earth slickening.

We didn't check the tide times before we left, and now it is too late. There is no mobile signal in the valley, no question of looking online. Generally speaking the state of the rocks, whether they are wet or dry, will at least indicate the direction of the tide – unless, of course, it is raining. It is no use trying to extrapolate from the sea's movements at Port Isaac yesterday. What I do know is this: I am soaked through, cold, and very, very hungry. The rain has infiltrated my anorak. My damp pullover feels horrible against my skin though it has a nostalgic smell, a faint lanolin oiliness. I think about the pasties in Shaun's backpack: they will be getting soggy too, in their grease-blotched paper bags. The depleted walls of the wreckers' cottage are no match for this downward rain. The only thing for it is to step down with the stream – careful now, it's slippery. CAREFUL!! – and splash and jump and clack our way across the cove, and eat our pasties in the shelter of the cave. The sea seems low enough, the waves breaking steadily at the tip of the slate slope. Maybe the rain will ease off soon.

The air in the cave is seagull breath. We perch on the ledge at the back and watch the weather as through a proscenium arch. If I crane my neck to look out and up, I can see the wreckers' cottage on the opposite edge. From here it looks more precarious than ever. My pasty is soggy and they've scrimped on the steak, but goodness it hits the spot.

Thunder split overhead without a warning rumble. It rico-
cheted around the sides of the cove, hard as rock and hollow
as nothing. The lightning simultaneous. One streak fizzled
close at hand, pure electricity. I love a good storm, but our cave
was beginning to feel a little on the shallow side. Shaun said
nothing. The wreckers' cottage was no longer visible for water
falling out of the sky. Amalgamated raindrops pelted on rocks
with a force that sent them skyward again. I was shivering now
with the cold and the wet, and huddled closer to Shaun. The
elemental outpouring.

The thunder and the pouring pounding rain. And, amongst
it all, a growing sound. I barely noticed it for a while, a galloping
rhythm overlaid with the whoosh of a seashell held to the ear.
All at once it was loud, within touching distance. The noise
resolved into cracks and thuds: solid sounds. Spray slammed
high close at hand, and hung for a moment in the raining air,
and fell heavily. Shaun stepped over to the mouth of the cave.
The sea was there, pressing into the cove. We grabbed our things
and made for the gulley.

A volume of brown water barrelled down where the stream
had been. It forced its way between the slate walls and burst out
into the cove. Flood tide and floodwater converged, everything
thundering as the sky thundered. By instinct, for the water was
rising fast, I climbed onto a rock. Come on, Shaun was saying,
we have to get out. That is when the special paralysis of the old
nightmare took over. The walls of rock, the advancing waves, the
grey sea like the grey sky closing in. I cannot move, I dreamed
back then, and in any case there is no way out. I am petrified,
turned to stone. My eight-year-old self had lost sleep in anticipation of this moment and, when sleep had eventually come,

rehearsed it in her dreams. It had come to pass: we were cut off. Behind me lay a lifetime, give or take, of seeking out corners and now, in my cove, in my safe place, Shaun and I were cornered.

My muscles continued to work without me: I kept my balance on the rock. Come on, Shaun was shouting, *no!* as I bent to unlace my walking boots. You keep your boots on and keep hold of my hand. We waded through the salty-muddy turbulence, feeling our way between rocks, over rocks, and then we climbed up into the gulley, the downward water, hugging the wall, over angles on which, when you can see them, you consider every step. The force of the water against my thighs and the instinct to maintain a counterforce, and the need to keep going, to get out of there – which, because we had to, we would do.

The sun was out by the time we got back to Port Isaac. We showered and changed into dry clothes, and then we went to the pub. We didn't talk about what had transpired in the previous hours. We drank pints of Tribute instead.

It was too soon to think about those events. I still tiptoe around them, and suspect I always will. I know that, while the flash flood could not have been predicted, we could and should have checked the tide times. I know, too, that we had been in danger and that it had felt like real danger. Did I fear for our lives? That I don't know. What happened in the cove that morning happened to us alone. Until now I have barely spoken about it for fear of being disbelieved, suspected of elaborating, for after all it is in the nature of anecdotes that they be honed. There is another reason, too. What happened frightened me so much that I do not want to believe it myself: it has both the vividness and the unreality of a terrible dream. And yet it happened.

When I next looked at Shaun's Ordnance Survey map, I saw

the picture of a flash flood in the making. The dense red gradient lines of the valleys, the blue meandering lines of the streams,
their tributaries and serial convergences. The high quarries betokening impermeable bedrock, runoff waiting to happen, and
the high boggy places around Treligga, Trebarwith, Trecarne;
the springs, the two valleys joining forces, all that confluence
heading for the cove. One stream rose in the hemlock grove. The
other had two sources, one of which rose more or less where the
tower should be.

The cove had scared the living daylights out of me. I'd experienced a terrifying vindication of my childhood fears, those
dark bedtime inventories of rocky places and incoming tides. I
thought about the Cornish chough and the large blue butterfly,
how both species had vanished from the cove around the time
of that dreadful *but*. How the *but* had muscled in between bedtime and sleep and, from three-hundred-and-eleven miles away,
involved my cove with fears too appalling to voice lest utterance
bring them to pass. That we would get cut off by a misjudged
tide, or slip off a narrow ledge, a high sheer edge, be brained by
rocks falling from an overhanging cliff. That my parents would
die, a weighty burden for an eight-year-old. Is everything going
to be alright? I asked my mother amongst the sobs.

Some things weren't, in the event, and some things were. My
mother died, far too young; so, too, did my father. And then,
though it stopped short of mortal realisation, the cove had set
about justifying the anxieties that darkened my nights in the
weeks before each longed-for Cornish holiday: every last slate-
coloured, inundating, obsorpating fear. I very nearly stepped off
that cliff, but not quite. A lump of rock dislodged by a seagull

almost smashed my head in, but not quite. And that last of my childhood prophecies, a scenario that came with its own dark cinematic set, had come to pass: Shaun and I had got cut off. But we survived. *But* is not such a terrible word.

Even so, the sum of these coincidences was a striking pattern. In moments of quiet free fall, especially at night, it took me to the brink of imagining that the cove, or something in or about the cove, were having to do with me. I'd teeter, the ground shifting, and step back: coincidences happen. A pattern does not presuppose significance, supernatural or otherwise. And yet . . . Then again these things were, if not waiting to happen, there for someone to happen to, for the cove is an unsettled place. The carved-out gulley, the gouged and precariously piled-up cliffs. And the weather, and the tides.

Of two things I am certain. Firstly, we ought to have checked the tide times. Secondly, I did not bring these fears to pass by articulating them: I was punctilious about that as my mother pleaded with me, all those years ago, to tell her what was wrong. Now that they have been as good as realised I find that I can speak freely about them. I don't have to worry about uttering them into probability, and I – Shaun and I – have lived to tell the tale.

The large blue butterflies died out, but maybe – just maybe – they will be back. And the choughs, one day, perhaps.

*

The phone rang one October morning. I was at my desk, watching the birds. I picked up. Silence. I held on, listening. Hello, a man's voice said at last, carefully, I think I've had a letter from you. Ah! Is that Mr Johnson? Ye-es. Well, it's Beth here. I thought it would be. Oh it's so good to hear from you, Mr Johnson – may I call you David? You can call me anything you like; now, about this letter of yours.

Following that walk in Treligga with Pete, it had taken me a long time to get around to writing to David, his farmer neighbour who, whether he liked it or not, now owned the tower and the asbestos-roofed accommodation blocks. Life had taken over, as it does, and our next, eventful trip to Cornwall (they all seemed to be eventful these days) was a flying one. I think I also assumed that any approach would quite reasonably be ignored or rejected as the intrusiveness of a holidaymaker, a species prone to causing problems for farmers and landowners. So I did nothing and then, one day, I fired off a letter: Dear Mr Johnson. His neighbour Pete had given me his address; we'd had a long chat when I was passing through Treligga some while back. I appreciated that I was contacting him out of the blue, and with an unusual request. I hoped he'd bear with me. I had been walking the coast path at the edge of his land, on and off, for most of my life. The cove had a special place in my heart, and I came back whenever I could. I was curious about the human stories that had shaped the place, and had recently found out about the old airfield. I'd seen the buildings from the top of the metal staircase and they intrigued me. Was there any chance that he might be willing to show me around one day? I should also mention that I'd been slightly obsessed with the observation tower since I was a child: for a good fifty years now I had dreamed of looking out from those second-floor windows, and it would mean the world to me to see it at closer quarters. I might even try to write a book about it all at some point.

David was happy to talk. Holidaymakers came in droves, he said, and he shouldn't complain because he ran lets himself, but visitors hardly ever took an interest in the people who actually lived and worked here. He told me that each of the fields on the farm once had a name. That the Admiralty had compulsorily purchased the land from his father in 1939, and sold it back in the early sixties in an altogether different state, the buildings, everything, left as was, eight of those named fields gone, the hedgebanks razed. The bomb craters and rusty detritus, spent rocket shells – they grubbed up a lorryload and sold it for scrap – and, not uncommonly, unexploded ordnance. Bits of rail from the tramway. The tramway? Yes, on the edge of the common. Not that long bank where the thyme and chamomile grew? I still liked to walk on it as children like to walk along low walls. Yes, that was the one: they installed a moving target later in the war to train pilots for conflict in the Pacific. The target was drawn by a locomotive, but it always seemed to be out of commission because when you hit the target it was hard to miss the rails.

Anyway, David said, he would gladly show us around when we were next down that way. And if I ever got around to writing that book he wanted to be in it. I hoped we might make it down before Christmas; maybe we could even rent one of his cottages for a few days. I thanked him sincerely, looked forward to meeting him soon. And – um – I didn't want to presume on his time and generosity – but did he think it might be at all possible for me to step inside the tower while we were there? He must be getting on, he said: goodbye.

I tried to picture a tramway along the clifftop where the chamomile grew and rabbit warrens crumbled to the sea. The tumuli diminished to bumps, their subterranean traces restored to privacy. The long, low, thyme-mottled bank, the gorse and the heather, the enamelled flowers, the salt wind into which I leaned, a peregrine taking shape in fog. The landscape that I knew and loved was just that, the landscape that I knew and loved. It was neither wild nor man-made, but a snapshot, a mere fifty-year moment, in the place's continuous story.

Shaun and I arrived at Treligga on a stormy evening in late November. We found the key under a designated piece of slate and let ourselves into a rather functional stable conversion. I loved the fact that animals once lived here, and that night I slept peacefully. Peace was to drift away into a clattering Atlantic gale, rain at the window like a lullaby, and wake late, happy. Happy because you have slept solidly for almost eight hours: you haven't done that since you don't know when, and to find that body and soul are still capable thereof is a wonderful thing. Happy upon recollecting where you are. Happy, and hungry – ravenous as a child, in fact – for the day ahead. There is sun beyond the bedroom curtains, sunshine after rain, and when you wander into the kitchen – Shaun is up, you can smell coffee – and look out of the little window, there will be a daub of sea in the middle distance.

An inexpressibly lovely day on the cusp of winter. David had said he'd call for us after lunch. That would be perfect, roughly what time? After lunch. We walked to Tregardock on streaming paths. The air warm and lively on my face, the sky so vivid that it might have been transmuted to a solid state. The low sun made everything more than itself, the sea blue deeper, the sky blue bluer, the fields green as fields in a children's book. At midday a pale moon hung overhead. We hurried back to make sandwiches and wondered what time David took lunch.

Sometime later he pulled up in a proper fieldfaring 4×4. There was only room for one passenger in the cab, so I perched on a wheel arch in the back and bumped about with loose straw and a pair of wellingtons. I thought of the Wrens arriving here in the backs of Bedford trucks. Hedgebanks, wind-sculpted thorns: the rearward vistas and the diesel fumes. We turned the corner by the tumbledown barn, the slate roof sprawled in its proper order, and I hopped down to open the gate to the old airfield.

We looked inside the hangar that once housed the fire engine and ambulance and now contained farm machinery. It smelled of engine oil and feed or fertiliser, stuff that comes in sacks. A pristine pigeon egg on the floor; dust swarming in a shaft of sun. We wandered on around the low buildings, slate and asbestos and bathtubs, brambles. I peered in at one window after another, toilets and more bathtubs, oxidised taps, a classic iron pull-chain cistern. Murk and indistinct clutter. Crunching asbestos. A doorway, partly boarded up, that gave onto a dark corridor; a ripple of old apprehension, something to do with a derelict house darkened by colossal rhododendrons. Aren't you coming inside? David said.

This room, David tells us, was the ship's mess. It is crammed with the detritus of its own dismantlement, and modern junk and bales of straw. In my mind's eye a black-and-white image displaces the chaos. Beneath that broken window an out-of-focus woman sits alone at a table, writing; her back is turned to me, and today she is more ghostly than ever. I wonder how she feels and what she is writing and, if to anyone, to whom. We move on to the kitchen, which is equally cluttered and murkier. There is the white-tiled stove surround: I've seen it before in a photograph, though the Rayburn and its shiny black flue are gone. Right here, in the place's memory, a woman is standing at a table, a white apron over her regulation shirt. She is rubbing fat and flour together, and her companion has just removed something from the phantom stove. Timber and broken glass and corroded window frames are piled up in the kitchen's present; massing ivy fills a hole in the asbestos roof. A corridor leads us deeper into the building. It is cold now, colder than the bright November day outside, and the place feels so desolate that you could almost think it sentient, believe it capable of having desolate feelings. Some of the fir-green doors are closed. We open them quietly, cautiously, as if afraid of what we might find inside, as if we are not supposed to be there at all, as if David doesn't own the property. As if it belongs, or also belongs, to somebody or something else; something listening.

Paintwork that once was pink has disintegrated, flaking to the colour and textures of lichen, strange curls accumulating on the floor. A door bears a faint trace of the word CABIN. It opens into a room of earthy yellow and evergreen trim, ivy pressing darkly in through broken windowpanes. David opens door after door. This was the communications room, this a darkroom. The corridor feels draughty and enclosed at once, and has a distinctive cold smell. Bare screed compounds the cold; locals liberated the linoleum, along with washbasins and most of the sinks, when the Admiralty left. We move on like ghosts amongst the remnants of past life. A rusted iron fuse box, that old radiator, light cables dangling bleakly from ceilings, Bakelite sockets and switches that make me think of my grandmother. I came in here on my own once, David says suddenly. It was just after they'd sold the place back to his father; it was around sunset, he was fifteen years old. And it was just, well. ??? I don't know, he says at last. It was just . . . spooky. You know, stuff. It just completely freaked me out.

Now we are in a dormitory. The colour of the walls has lost itself between pink and yellow and there is no sign of the chintz curtains that suggested cosiness in the photograph. But on the walls, at bed-width intervals, two wire hooks and a green wooden shelf have every appearance of readiness for coats and dressing gowns and personal effects. A wardrobe, on the other hand, stands a little apart from its wall in an attitude of absolute abandonment. The veneer hangs off in flayed greyed strips, but the trim is solid and intricately carved with berries and leaves in the Arts and Crafts style. This room faces west. It smells and feels warmer, different from the other spaces through which we have passed. It must be the light, and the residual trappings of a room in which young women hung their clothes and did their hair, swapped lipsticks and life stories; had worries and heartbreaks and were homesick; gossiped and messed around, and slept. It is as if the walls themselves are somehow conscious of these things: as if the place, remembering, waits and listens still.

Something crunches under my foot. This time it is not asbestos, but a scattering of owl pellets. David picks one up and breaks it open to show us the tiny mouse bone inside.

As we retrace our steps through the building I try to place the piano, the foxgloves and the jug. I am sure I would see them, summon them up, if I could stay here just a little bit longer, but

David is waiting in the doorway. Maybe there will be another time.

Out into the brilliance. The blue sea and the land's lovely sweep to Rumps Point. We waded through rough grass: the kitchen garden – I'd read that the Wrens had particular success with cabbages – and, marked by two rusty posts, the tennis court. Beyond lay a grassed-over mound with a dark entrance beneath a concrete lintel. It was clearly an air-raid shelter but brought to mind a prehistoric barrow, its portal not yet sealed upon the dead. You'd better go in, David said, we'll wait up here. Down inside it was strangely fresh. I tried to imagine the space without its brick and concrete revetments. One wall bore a white-painted heart and arrow – HAPPY DAYS. AUG. 48. – and, at the top, two mud swallow nests, one fairly recent. Another angle between wall and ceiling was densely colonised by snails. It looked as if some belated Victorian had started to build a shell grotto and thought better of it.

We drove off again, over fields, accelerating into the sun. Gossamer threaded through the grass in parallel lines. I was looking forwards now, peering through the tiny window between the men's heads; they were talking animatedly. There was nothing but sun, and then there was the tower. It stood amongst mud and enormous puddles that, reflecting the cloudless sky, drained the brickwork of solidity and presented it as mirage.

Used there not to be an external staircase? I asked. Indeed there was, David said, the sheep used to climb it; eventually he'd bricked it in. He lifted the door open – the tongue-and-groove was rotten, ragged – and at last, unbelievably, I stepped inside the tower.

The first thing I felt was crushing disappointment. The brick walls of the wartime photographs were lined with plasterboard. Pipes and ducting lay about awaiting connection, and new cables hung from ceilings and walls, a strange reflection of the derelict muddle from which we had just come. I wanted the interior of my tower to have been left untouched: it was a tower in a clifftop field, it needed windows, that was all. Still, I had come to look out of those windows and I'd waited nearly half a century to do so. Would it be OK if I were to step straight up to the second floor?

The vistas at which my imagination had worked for so long did not allow for such mundanities as plaster dust and finger-prints, smudges and desiccated drips; multitudes of flies, some dead, some buzzing; and, on the other side, relentless lashings of Atlantic salt. The Wrens would have kept the windows of their tower crystal clear, an operational responsibility of greater weight than mere good housekeeping. But here I was, after all these years, on the top floor of the tower, in a corner with two windows, one of which faced the cove and the other North America. I can't wait to tell Mum about this, I caught myself feeling, almost thinking. I looked west first. The grubby glass reduced what lay beyond to generalities. A strip of grey had formed at the horizon. Above it was sky, below it sea and, below the sea, green land. To my eye it curved very slightly, like the earth. I turned to the north-facing window but David was there, ushering me on, into a tiny room crammed with building mate-rials. A small cupboard door was set into one wall. Go on then, David said, nodding towards it, take a look. I opened the door. Sunlight poured down a wooden staircase. I climbed over a sack of plaster and ducked through the aperture: forget Narnia, this was the real deal. Shaun was behind me. Don't get mud on my new stairs, David shouted. I was on the top step, pushing at a skylight. My boots were muddy, I realised too late. The skylight was high, and heavy. I hauled myself, wriggling, up and out.

Shaun and I are standing on the roof of the tower. The sun is making dials of us. Our shadows stretch east-north-east, telling their own time. I breathe in everything I see with the salty wind. *This.* In the distance beyond Rumps Point a suggestion of coast continues like a pencil line, and fades. I grip Shaun's hand and look, and look, west into infinity. *The light. The ocean. All of it.*

I cross the roof towards the sea. One step more to look over the edge. Mud and puddles hurtle towards me and my insides shift about. I stand back, everything spinning. Shaun is shouting at me.

A spring rises below the tower on the northern side. Gorse and perfect stunted thorns describe its course, a few dots growing to a fluent thread. The scrub gains momentum as it thickens downhill, the grassed depression deepening, dropping and merging to a stream that carves and angles and merges again in that cumulative course to the sea.

Here, on top of the world with Shaun, happiness possesses me. The slanting sun has dream-like intensity. We observe ourselves cast onto brilliant grass, an elongated shadow couple standing on a shadow tower. I map the trajectory of the spring, follow it down into the valley, the cove drawing me ineluctably. I watch my shadow move towards the edge of the roof as if somnambulant. I watch Shaun's shadow watch over mine.

*

Days touched with strangeness followed this charmed afternoon. The next morning, before dawn, I drove Shaun to Bodmin for his train to London. The end of the night was dark and clear. Back at the cottage I made a mug of tea and stood at the kitchen window. A light bobbed out at sea until the day lightened. Clouds moved in. Later, when I opened the front door, a robin hopped in and made an unhurried circuit of the living room, and left again. I walked to Tregardock in a soft sea drizzle. The bare-boned thorns, their leftover berries, darkening haws and shrivelled sloes. I climbed up behind The Mountain and took the path north. The tower was remote again, merged with grey. It was hard to believe that the previous day had happened at all.

I rang David to thank him. I wished him well with the rest of the work, hoped we could stop by to take a look when it was finished. The work? The renovation work – the tower. Oh, the tower. I don't think I'll be going into the tower again. What, never? No, never. I let the matter drop. I really don't know how to thank you for yesterday, I said, I just can't tell you what it meant to me, and to Shaun of course; I'll remember that afternoon for as long as I live. So will I, David said: it was really magical.

I stayed on at the cottage for four more nights. The days stretched and contracted and seeped as days do when you are alone and have nothing scheduled, and they darkened with the weather. I returned to the cove endlessly by one route or another. The valley was stripped to its essential shapes and greens, rusts, purples: winter on the way. There was no question of getting down to the cove; the gulley was running water. I haunted the edges of the place. The sea grew more agitated with each day, and powerful winds funnelled up the valley. Perched on my ledge in driving rain – the worst thing about getting wet is the getting wet; once you are soaked through it matters less – I watched the sea heave and drag enormously, terribly, working at the slate cliff where men once worked at it, finding out its weaknesses. Once, climbing up past the wreckers' cottage, I could have sworn that I smelled coal smoke on the wind. Once, as the day brightened just before dusk, starlings murmurated at the top of the valley in a twisting, tumbling, shape-shifting mass. Once I stood out beyond the tumuli and listened to an unsettled rock below; it cracked like gunfire when the waves took a certain powerful turn. I thought of limpets spawning in the turbulence.

On my last afternoon I misjudged the time, and when I headed back along the cliff path dusk was growing like a palpable thing. I was hurrying, worrying, a little out of breath. And then a light flashed beyond Rumps Point, and again, and on a count of seven again, and on the next count a gigantic lantern flashed above the headland. The light's form conjured, magnified, by an inversion of temperature: a superior mirage in every sense. I waited, transfixed. The lantern flashed twice more on successive counts, and then the lighthouse resumed its far-off blink. I thought about the rainbows in the Fresnel lenses, an earliest memory burning bright. Long walks around Trevose Head with my mother, the gales and the evening sky, putting the world to rights. Sitting on Trevose Head one evening with Shaun, the dusk deepening and the lighthouse light brightening. It was getting dark but I was high on enchantment. I'd find my way home.

*

I did not open the little plastic boxes of slides that illustrate my childhood for many years after the deaths of my parents. Maybe I was afraid that I would feel too much or, worse, not enough. Then, on impulse, a good four decades after the last family slide show, I bought an ancient viewer for next to nothing in a charity shop. I rather expected the bulb to have blown, but when I put in batteries and pressed the switch the screen lit up. I do not know what I expected next.

Shared memory is a precious thing: it nourishes the story of who you are. Shaun and I have a memory pool that is twenty-seven years deep, and counting. But the slides from my childhood belong to a memory of many parts that deaths and scatterings have lessened. Untested and unrenewed by others who were there – who might infill, contextualise, explain, disagree – my own memory is by turns vivid and uncertain of itself, moving around spaces into which corresponding shapes never got to be fitted. There wasn't time; there never is. As each slide clicks and is illuminated, so familiar but so strange – so far off, so long ago – I scrutinise each face including my own, looking and feeling for connection; photographs need more than themselves if they are to stay alive. And I think again of de la Mare's Traveller, the 'one man left awake', feeling in his heart the listeners' 'strangeness', the 'stillness' with which they answer him.

A remarkable thing happened around this time. I discovered that I wanted to share the cove with others – with our family of friends. Shaun and I were in South Cornwall, eating pasta from mismatching plates with our friends Angie and Nick and Sam, who was three-and-a-half years old and proud of it. It was mid-August; they'd invited us into their holiday for a few precious nights. That cove of yours, Nick said suddenly, when are you taking us there? How about tomorrow? An old instinct kicked in. My ears ringing, my vision gone. It lasted the merest fraction of a moment, but it was real: panic.

It was almost forty years to the week since I had set off for secondary school and fear set into my everyday life. It had never occurred to me that I might share my cove with anyone other than Shaun; on the contrary, I was habitually secretive about the place. In adulthood it cropped up in conversations with friends – it couldn't not – but if somebody pressed me regarding its precise location I practised vagueness and moved the conversation along. It made no sense, for I knew that anyone could find the cove on a map, or chance upon it when walking the coast path. I recognised, albeit with distaste, that all kinds of people could and did go to the cove whenever they wished; then again, fear does not deal in logic. My farmer friends didn't count, because they lived there.

My cove was sacrosanct. It was my safe, happy place, and as I grew up it became absolutely imperative to keep it safe. Safe, untainted, which was to say, secret. I patrolled its boundaries rigorously. Just to mention the cove at school would be to compromise, sully it. Should I fail to maintain that separation, if anyone on the school premises should get to hear of the cove, anything might happen. Even at the outermost extreme of anxiety, which admittedly was extreme, I did not believe – at least not quite, at least I do not think I did – that one or more of my tormentors would turn up at the cove as they had turned up at our garden gate, but that was not the point. If you are bullied for long enough, if you retreat, terrified, often enough, you come to mistrust friendliness itself. I found ways of not telling anyone, not even my golden-hearted potter friend nor the kind fifth formers, where we were going for half-term. I learned to be evasive. While it was the most natural thing in the world to take Shaun to the cove, old habits of self-preservation stuck.

Don't worry if you have other plans, said Angie, picking up on a flicker of doubt, we can always go on Wednesday instead. Goodness no, I'd love to do that tomorrow: that would mean the world to me. I meant it, I discovered there and then, from the bottom of my heart. Where are we going? Sam wanted to know. To the cove, we said in unison.

The weather was picture-postcard perfect, high pressure in charge. I'd checked the tide times twice before we left Fowey, and Angie had packed a picnic. Merriment prevailed, on the whole, in the crowded car. Are we nearly at the cove? asked Sam as we drove around St Austell. Where's the cove? he enquired at Bodmin, exasperated. But where's the *cove*? he demanded with good reason when, turning into the lane to Tregardock, I touched the brake and pointed out the patch of absolute blue ahead: *there's the sea! I can see the sea!*

We set off together down the track, into the blackthorns, up behind The Mountain, the heather and the gorse. Now, on the coast path, Angie and I have fallen behind. We have been stopping to look at the sea and smell warmed gorse flowers, their coconut intensity; to fiddle around, take photographs, give bits of conversation our undivided attention. I show Angie a hollow at the edge of the cliff where thyme blooms more brightly than anywhere else and bees cling on for dear life in gales. We talk about the ways to Rumps Point and Tintagel. Rough Tor, a place that Angie loves, due east below the inland horizon. I persuade her to taste a wild carrot flower. The men are some way across the common now. Sam is riding high on Nick's shoulders, just as I once rode this way on my father's shoulders, and I know that the little boy is on top of the world. The tower over there in its great green space. I tell Angie how, after decade upon decade of longing, I'd climbed to the top this past November, and how she would not believe what I saw. Angie thinks the tower is on the small side, but says she gets my fascination. On the common we stop again to kneel and smell chamomile. The sun-pressed scent is drowsy, beguiling: unbelievable.

By the time we reach the top of the valley the others are at the bottom. They have crossed the slate-stone bridge and are heading straight for the villa foundation. According to my yellow booklet the tide should still be fairly high, but the cormorants' rock seems a little more exposed than it ought, a fringe of brown wrack visible above the water level. It must be one of those low high tides, something to do with the time of the month or fair-weather pressure. There are two cormorants on the rock, looking west past Puffin Island, and their wings are folded tight against their sleek bodies. Normally, I tell Angie, they are outstretched: cruciform, showing me things. Sam is busy with flowers and nooks, noticing, exclaiming; his voice carries joyfully. Now the three of them are standing on the seaward edge of the villa. Shaun and Nick are deep in conversation, the little boy is gazing out to sea, and they are right on the edge of the cliff, and because of the treacherous thrift they cannot see the danger they are in. I can see it all. The low cliff is high enough and there are rocks below. Shaun! Nick! Get back from the edge, I shout inside but no words come. This sort of thing happens in nightmares yet I am awake. Shaun throws his head back, laughing, and lurches slightly. I am watching and am paralysed. Get back, *get back*, I think to them. My voice and my feet may not respond to the frantic signals from my brain, but surely in a moment of such extremity I can influence these people whom I love and who are in danger before my eyes. GET BACK, I think harder. Later I will have no idea how long this moment has lasted; it is said that long narratives and complex scenarios are dreamed in split seconds.

The men turn around slowly, chatting still, and amble away from the edge, and stretch out in the sun on the grassy platform at the centre of the earthwork. It's an excellent spot for a picnic. Sam is investigating a corner of the ditch. It is interesting, and deep enough; he is safe. Angie is ahead of me. Everything is set out in full view below, but she gives no indication that she has seen what I have just seen. I must hurry to catch up with her. I want to show her the wreckers' cottage. Maybe there will be a whiff of coal smoke, maybe not. Maybe I'll tell her about the dead cow, maybe not. Then we will join the others, settle down on the grass in the sun, and Angie will unpack a feast from a rucksack of seemingly infinite capacity.

Maybe, just maybe, when the tide goes out, we will step down beside the stream, the little boy on his father's shoulders, over the tilting slate into the cove, into the future of my cove.

*

It would be some time before I saw the cove again. The following spring Covid-19 turned the world upside down. Time went into lockdown too, passing at a measureless pace: it stood still, it went in a flash. Once in a while, as I fiddled with a piece of slate or Shaun was asking if I'd heard from Pete and Sandra lately, my phone would ping with a photograph from the top of Pete's field, the postcard view over Treligga. Or it would ring and Pete would say I was just thinking about you both, thought I'd check in. On one such occasion he was calling with the sad news that David had died suddenly. I still think about my last conversation with David – how, following that magical afternoon, he had told me he would not be setting foot in the tower again.

I longed for the cove, longed to be there. I thought and felt my way along the cliff path: the gorse, the church in and out of sight, the tower, the heather, the rabbit holes. Out onto the headland, the tumuli, the idea of Atlantic wind, steep down now, the cove there below, the wreckers' cottage, down by the stream – carefully, carefully – one step at a time. One night at the edge of sleep I lost my footing on the slippery slate, and falling jolted wide awake. On down to the foot of the gulley, searching for cool mineral smells, out into the rocky light. Listening hard for the cove's special echo, the sound of the cove listening. I dug deep for churned seaweed in the surface of a wave, for something pungent and salt-vegetal. Deeper still for the sounds of the sea, its lapping, colliding, breaking, wearing, shaping dance with the rocks and the cliffs. But the cove that sustained me was an amalgam of sensory memories. I needed to hear it for myself, for itself, to smell smells that were the cove's alone. Feel the textures of its rocks beneath my hands and knees; look into a pool that was not a composite rock pool, but a living, glinting ecosystem.

When at last, two years later, we drove downhill to the Tamar bridge, the car gaining speed like an eager thing – CORNWALL: KERNOW, the window rolled down – over the river, and Shaun said, we're back, I breathed in deeply. Tomorrow I would go to the cove, and the day after.

It is in the nature of the cove that nothing is set in stone. In our absence part of the gulley wall had collapsed and dumped an avalanche of slate to one side of the stream. The quarried rockface, weakened, had continued to weaken behind the scenes and given way suddenly, spectacularly. It had tumbled and fractured, with who knows what noise, into more-or-less rhomboid solids that looked for all the world as though they had been cut. It will happen again one day, next year or next century, next millennium. One day the days of stepping down by the stream will instantly be over.

And, hurrying along the path to my ledge, I stopped and stepped back, and closed my eyes until the wave of sickness passed. Then I set off again, levering myself with a walking pole into the grassy cliff side, my eyes averted from the rocks below, the path edge and the air between them, concentrating on the grass. Was it me, grown timid in that time away, out of touch with the ways of the cove, or was it the path? Safely across the narrow bit I stopped and looked back. It was definitely the path; at least, I think it was. No one in their right mind would walk along that.

Hello cove. I heard the sea shift underwater rocks as though moving furniture about. A loud crack every now and then: an unsettled rock, the unsettled waves. Their collisions and rip currents, localised slurpings. I watched them work at the cliffs and the rocks and listened as they milled the shingle, dragged tiny slates and beads of quartz into new configurations, softened the contours of quarried rocks, refining them still. No, nothing here is set in stone.

I am not sure I have ever known the tide so low. It must have something to do with the moon. Yesterday evening we sat out on the headland and watched the west long into the afterglow: a ceremonious time of day, the world stilling. The sea shifted quietly below. Seabirds were settling with self-contained, residual calls. A hawk perched next to us on a lump of slate. It was still as stone, and its bright eyes were inscrutable. When I turned around a giant moon had risen at our backs. Shaun and I almost always disagree about a waxing moon: at some point one of us declares it full and the other insists that it isn't quite. Last night the moon was full enough.

Shaun has waded off into tangle, and though he has almost reached the cormorants' rock the water is barely at his knees. The tide is so low and the cove so still. Almost too still: the air of restraint is palpable, as if the place were holding its breath, listening hard. I can hear the muted grunts of the cormorants. The wide pale pools, the crystalline light, the absolute calm could be the cove dreamed – though a limpet point feels real enough to my bare instep, and the back of my neck is tingling in the salt sun. I do not know if it is possible to dream in such detail.

I am treading on across the rocks, on and on around the base of the cliff. Where I am going it is easy to forget the time and tide – but the water is so low, I have to keep going, and I know that Shaun will call me when the tide turns. My feet arch slowly, deliciously over slate. The threads and seams of cold white quartz. The sea's there-sound. It has been years since I came so far; these parts are cut off more often than not. But there, beneath the shallow waves amongst the rocks, is wavy sand. The water is lit with a kind of pale interior blue. Moon jellyfish are bobbing.

You wade into the miniature waves: they are chill, and they agitate at your calves, and drag. Your bare feet remember the undulations, sand made wave-like by the waves as gravel is made wave-like by a Zen gardener's rake. The sand flows on out of the water into a recess, a cove within the cove. The west, the sun, the ocean at your back. Maybe, if you look hard enough, you will catch sight of your mother: she is sitting, gazing out to sea as you wade towards the shore. The rocks are wave-smooth and warmed by the sun: you could sit down here and forget yourself.

The metamorphic listening slate.

The towering mutilated cliff, slate projecting from an edge.

A cormorant, its gesturing wings: *this. The light. The salt-bright light. The ocean. All of it.*

I do not think that lump of slate will fall today.

Acknowledgements

Thank you to my editor Jenny Lord and my agent Jessica Woollard. To Lucinda McNeile for painstaking editorial support; to my copyeditor Simon Fox; and to Esme Bright and Georgia Glover at David Higham. A special thank you to Andy Lovell for the exquisite cover illustration.

My thanks also go to the staff of the Maps Room at Cambridge University Library; Hannah Curnow and Sara Homes of Cornwall County Council; Ben Dixon of the Natural History Mueum; Mike Simmonds of the National Trust; and Steve Perry of the Cornwall at War Museum.

I am full of gratitude to the following people for all manner of help and encouragement along the way: Alec and Cheryl Clements; Colin and Diana Davey; Graham and Jeanette Elston; Bob and Cathryn Franklin; Daphne Hall; Roberta Melchior; Mole Piotrowicz; Anita Thomas; Jerry Toner; and Huw Williams.

The writing of this book would have been a different businesss without the immense generosity of Carol Clift and Anne Toner. I am indebted to these two wise women.

Shaun, my huge-hearted husband, has lived with this project for longer than either of us might have wished. He has supported me unstintingly, in ways that I cannot begin to enumerate. I can only thank him for his kindness; for walking with me; for everything.

Works Cited

Armitage, Simon, *Walking Away* (London: Faber & Faber, 2015)

Beard, Richard, *The Day That Went Missing* (London: Harvill Secker, 2017)

Betjeman, John, *Cornwall: A Shell Guide* (London: Faber & Faber, 1964)

Causley, Charles, *Collected Poems 1951–2000*, revised edition (London: Picador, 2000)

Christie, Patricia M., 'Barrows on the North Cornish Coast: Wartime Excavations by C.K. Croft Andrew 1939–1944', *Cornish Archaeology* 24 (1985), 23–121

Collins, Wilkie, *Rambles Beyond Railways* (London: Richard Bentley, 1851)

Craze, Neil, Peter Herring & Graeme Kirkham, 'Atlantic Coast and Valleys Project: Historic Environment Assessments of Farms' (Cornwall County Council, 2006)

De la Mare, Walter, *Collected Poems* (London: Faber & Faber, 1942)

Du Maurier, Daphne, *Jamaica Inn* [1936] (Harmondsworth: Penguin, 1972)

Handbook for Travellers in Devon and Cornwall, A [1851], fourth edition, revised (London: John Murray, 1859)

Hardy, Emma, *Some Recollections*, revised edition (Oxford: Oxford University Press, 1979)

Hardy, Thomas, *A Pair of Blue Eyes* [1873] (Oxford: Oxford University Press, 2005)

——, *The Life and Work of Thomas Hardy*, ed. by Michael Millgate (London: Palgrave Macmillan, 1984)

——, *The Complete Poems*, ed. by James Gibson (London: Macmillan, 1976)

Hauck, Dennis William, *The International Directory of Haunted Places* (New York: Penguin Putnam, 2000)

Methuen, Algernon, ed., *An Anthology of Modern Verse* [1921], seventh school edition (London: Methuen & Co., 1924)

Norden, John, *Speculi Britanniae Pars: A Topographical and Historical Description of Cornwall* [1728], facsimile (Newcastle-upon-Tyne: Frank Graham, 1966)

Page, Norman, ed., *Tennyson: Interviews and Recollections* (London: Macmillan, 1983)

Provis, Geoff, *The Fishermen of Port Isaac* (Launceston: Trefeock Publications, 2009)

Shakespeare, William, *The Tragedy of Macbeth* [1623], ed. by Nicholas Brooke (Oxford: Oxford University Press, 2008)

Sharpe, Adam, *Coastal Slate Quarries: Tintagel to Trebarwith* (Truro: Cornwall County Council, 1990)

Tennyson, Hallam, *Alfred Lord Tennyson: A Memoir*, Volume 1 [1897] (Cambridge: Cambridge University Press, 2012)

Tomlinson, Jill, *The Owl Who Was Afraid of the Dark* [1968] (Harmondsworth: Puffin, 1973)

Trollope, Anthony, *An Autobiography* [1883] (Oxford: Oxford University Press, 1980)

——, *Lotta Schmidt and Other Stories* [1867] (Harmondsworth: Penguin, 1993)

'Waller, Fi' (pseud.), *Wrens in King Arthur's Country* (Cheltenham: privately printed, 1999)

Note

I have retained original spelling in all quotations except for the 'v' in early-modern texts; this has been silently standardised. Some names have been changed.